NO SHIRT
NO SHOES
NO SERVICE

NO SHIRT
NO SHOES
NO SERVICE

STEVE COX

© 2013 Steve Cox

All rights reserved. No part of this publication may be reproduced, distributed, or transmitted in any form or by any means, including photocopying, recording, or other electronic or mechanical methods, without the prior written permission of the publisher, except in the case of brief quotations embodied in critical reviews and certain other noncommercial uses permitted by copyright law.

The events of this story are true, but some names have been changed in the interest of privacy.

Edited by Sarah Cypher
Book design by Phillip Gessert

I dedicate this book to my late wife, Barbara.

CHAPTER 1

It was a hot summer night and Lewis and I didn't have much to do. We didn't set out in search of mayhem, but sometimes it found us—and usually at the center of town. That night, we met up with some friends in a parking lot between Gilly's Candy and Dawson's Hardware. Our only desire was to vacate our homes and get away from our parents. At Gilly's, at least back then, you could buy six candy bars for a quarter. Invariably, some friends would show up and meet us there, and we'd usually move on to score some beer, cool off skinny-dipping at Hood's Pond, and just hang out.

My friend Jimmy Bishop lived a few miles from the town center and across the street from Hood's Pond. Jim's family owned a gas station and convenience store next to the small, three-bedroom house he shared with nine siblings and his mom and dad. Beer was easy to come by at Jim's house because his elder brothers and sisters were old enough to buy it for us. The last time we were there, a few of us lay on our backs on the roof of the house drinking beer and watched the Perseids. Every time we saw the bright white tail of a shooting star careening through the upper atmosphere, we gave a whooping cheer. The loudness of our appreciation was proportional to the brilliance and duration of the meteor, multiplied by the number of beers consumed. We had a good time up there on the roof.

So, Jimmy Bishop, Lewis, and I found each other that evening in the town center looking for camaraderie and adolescent entertainment. Lewis and I were finalizing the plans for our big trip. We talked it up to our friends as a cross-country journey, but we really planned to just drive to Colorado and then back home to Topsfield, Massachusetts. Also, Jim had some beer hidden in his brother's pickup, which was parked behind Gilly's. The evening was off to a good start.

Behind the strip mall at the town center were the Proctor School, the town common, a church, and the police station. Proctor is the elementary school where Jim and I began our friendship. Fittingly, we had been bending rules together for just as long. Behind the school was the playground, and at the end of the playground was a small, camel hump of a hill. The hill looked out of place. It was as if someone had dumped a load of dirt there, except that the pile was about forty feet high and took up about half a football field at its base. The mound was populated with trees and shrubs, which made it good cover—people on the playground down below couldn't spot us up on the hill.

Contrarily, the hill was a good place to keep any eye on what was happening below. There were plenty of gaps in the vegetation to get a clear view of the swing sets and baseball diamonds. On the far edge of the playground, behind home plate, was a municipal building that housed the police station. It was an old wooden Victorian structure built back in the 1800s, bearing a century's worth of white paint. Up above the police station was where dances were held for the teenage crowd on Friday nights.

Back in the parking lot, Lewis, Jim, and I weren't about to let the beer get warm and go to waste. With libations in tow, the three of us decided the hilltop would be a discreet place to relax and drain some of the bottles. Off we went. It was dark under the trees at the top, but from the streetlights down below and the moon above, there was enough ambient light filtering through the vegetation for us to see. We had a good view of the school, the playground, and the police station from our vantage point.

Before long, two other friends found us sitting around the now-half-empty case of beer. Rick Evans, a few years older than us, ventured up the trail to the hilltop with a buddy we didn't recognize. But because they brought their own stash of beer, we welcomed them. At first, Rick's friend didn't say much. He just drank his beer and smoked cigarettes, as the rest of us all chatted in quiet voices, aware that the police station wasn't far away.

Voices drifted up to the hilltop. There was an abandoned railroad bed behind us, and it had become a well-worn path for pedestrians who wanted to take a shortcut through town. We knew to clam up until we were certain they were beyond earshot—and now, there were two people strolling along the path down below.

Rick reached into his pocket and pulled out an M80 and said to his friend, "Give me your cigarette so I can light this and toss it down behind those meatheads down there. It'll scare the shit out of 'em."

Lewis whispered to Rick, "Not a good idea. They will know it came from up here, and the police will probably hear it, too." Rick frowned at Lewis but took his advice and re-pocketed the firecracker.

It was getting close to midnight. We were running low on beer and were long on boredom. The crickets were chirping and there wasn't even a hint of a breeze. We were about to disband to find some other place to go when Rick said, "I have an idea." He reached in his pocket and pulled out his handful of M80s. "Let's wake up the police station!"

The rest of us laughed, not knowing if we should take his suggestion seriously.

"Let's light these things off around the station," he insisted.

"Are you crazy?" I said. "They'll catch us."

Rick reached over and grabbed the lit cigarette from his friend's mouth and said, "No, stupid, we'll make delayed fuses with cigarettes and plant them around the cop station. We'll have plenty of time to hide."

The rest of us sat and stared at each other for a few seconds as the idea sunk in. As the blank facial expressions slowly morphed into shit-eating grins, we all turned our heads in the direction of the municipal building. There, across an acre of field, were the front steps. Lit up by streetlights, there were two police cruisers parked along the striped pavement. The lights were on inside the station, illuminating the entire first floor. All indications were that there were constables in the building. If we were to give them a midnight surprise, we'd have to be very careful—or very lucky.

Looking across the field from the hilltop, the back of the school was at the two o'clock position. Home plate of the baseball diamond and the back of the police station were at ten o'clock. There were dark shadows behind the school all the way to the back of the police station, and from the base of the hill to the back wall of the school. If we stayed in the shadows, and close to the back wall of the school, we might be able to approach the station undetected.

Rick took the pack of cigarettes from his friend. He picked a twig up off the ground and poked a hole through a cigarette, close to where the tobacco ended and the filter started. In the hole made by the twig he pushed through the fuse of an M80. Rick made three cigarettes like this, attaching M80s to each one. After a cigarette had been lit, it would take a few minutes before the ember would make its way through the tobacco and ignited the fuse—just enough time for the pyrotechnician to get back to the hilltop to watch the reaction.

Lewis, Jim, and I remained on the hilltop as Rick and his buddy slipped down the hillside until they reached the shadows at the base. We glimpsed them as they made their way to the school. We could barely track their progress as they were crouched over and moving briskly along the back wall. They came to a break in the shadows between the school and the rear of the police station, and we held our breath as they darted between shadows.

They made it. About thirty tense seconds passed as they waited to see if they had been spotted. Or maybe they were deciding where to plant the bombs. The three of us on the hill saw a match light up behind the station. It was quickly covered by a pair of hands. They had lit the first cigarette. We learned later that they used the ember on the first lit cigarette to light the other two. They would hold a cigarette in their mouth and touch the lit end of one to light the end of the other, in between cupped hands.

Now, my adrenaline was starting to kick in. My senses sharpened and time seemed to slow down. After what seemed like too much time, we saw Rick and his friend sprinting from shadow to shadow, retracing the path they had first taken to ground zero. The bushes on the hill started to shiver, and then they emerged through the vegetation. They were back.

Out of breath, Rick said, "Mission accomplished."

Suddenly we heard a loud explosion. Followed quickly by a second. Rick had placed the first two M80 cigarettes under the front steps of the police station. Wide eyed, we all just watched silently from our hilltop hideout across the field.

The door of the police station burst open and cops poured out like a swarm of angry bees. Crouched over, they all ran into the parking lot, frantically looking to and fro. Just then the third M80 ignited and blew up like a stick of dynamite. It was under one of the police cruisers.

The cops all dove for cover on their bellies. One or two lay between the cruisers and the rest went for the dirt beside the road. The five of us on the hill were near bursting with laughter. It was all I could do to hold it in. The mere thought of the consequences of getting caught gave me the strength to stay quiet, though, and the other guys must have had the same thoughts, because they stifled their laughter, too.

Jerry Campbell, a redheaded classmate who lived just a few houses up the street, must have heard the commotion.

He appeared, pedaling his bicycle out of the shadows in the road. One of the cops who was cowering between two cruisers leaped up and tackled Jerry as he rode by. Jerry was knocked off his bicycle and onto the ground by the side of the road. The other officers ran over and pounced on him. They literally picked him up, carried him over and held him face down across the trunk of one of the cruisers.

Poor Jerry! Talk about being in the wrong place at the wrong time. The hilltop gang silently kept watching as the police stood Jerry up and interrogated him. I felt a bit sorry for the trouble we had caused him, but knowing Jerry, he'd have a nicely embellished story to tell his friends the next day.

Finally one of the officers walked over, picked up the bike, and handed it back to Jerry. Realizing he wasn't the perpetrator, they sent him on his way.

The hill was our grandstand. This was an even better show than we could have hoped for. We high-fived each other.

Before long, the police gave up their search around the station and retreated back into their barracks. Jerry was probably at home licking his wounds. We had consumed all of the beer and we could not think of any mischief that could top what we had already created. Rick and his friend departed. Jim, Lewis and I walked the railroad path back to downtown. A few minutes later Jim said his goodbye and drove off in his brother's truck. Lewis and I paused for a few minutes of reflection in the parking lot.

Before heading our separate ways we agreed to meet in the morning. Our cross-country trip, the one we had bragged about to all of our friends, was to start tomorrow. The thought gave me butterflies. Tomorrow we'd pack Lewis' car for the road trip, and be on our way towards the biggest adventure yet.

CHAPTER 2

It was the summer of 1971. We had survived the sixties—that decade of decadence, enlightenment, and experimentation, punctuated with a raging war in Vietnam that not many people my age could embrace as justified. I had friends who never came home, and others who came home minus body parts. I had just graduated from high school and turned eighteen a month before. Lewis had spent his first year at Michigan State University.

The sixties were over, but had not yet relinquished control of the times. My blond hair was shoulder length, so was Lewis's. More than once, people had asked if we were brothers. Lewis was a few inches taller than me and lankier, though we were both lean enough that our blue jeans and T-shirts hung off of us. His dad was living in a small one-bedroom apartment in Amesbury, Massachusetts, but Lewis was working that summer for his Uncle Richard, a mason who lived on the same property as Lewis's grandmother. His dad paid his grandma twenty dollars a week for Lewis's room and board.

It was August and the summer was heating the sidewalks. The New England weather in 1971 was typical of the time of year: searing sunshine, humidity, and long slow breezy days. Lewis and I were packing his American Motors 1963 Rambler station wagon. The wagon was parked in the front yard of his grandmother's house. The lawn had turned to a light brown color of straw by the sun; bordering the cracked asphalt driveway were overgrown bushes, and the thorns stabbed at us as we squeezed between the bushes and the car while loading camping equipment. The back seat had filled up with pots and pans, a camping stove, a tent, spare footwear, fishing gear—everything that two teenagers could think of as being essential for a summer adventure, including plenty of just-in-case items.

It wouldn't be until later on in life that I learned to pack what you think you need for travel, and then take half of it.

Lewis had purchased the Rambler station wagon for three hundred dollars from an old guy who couldn't drive anymore. It was on the wrong side of the eighty-thousand-mile-mark, and about the same color as his grandmother's grass, in two shades of brown—tan on the outside and light yellow on the inside. We nicknamed it the Bumblebee. It had a manual transmission with three on the column. Most people under fifty will have no idea what that means, but it was not uncommon back then. The car's only distinguishing feature was that you could slide the front seat forward and lower it far enough to make a fairly comfortable surface for two adults to sleep on. We'd decided it would make the perfect road trip car.

The trip to Colorado had been planted a summer earlier.

I had attended the Colorado Outward Bound School. Outward Bound was a month-long expedition, on foot, through the Rocky Mountain Wilderness. It was one of the most physically challenging experiences of my life. The goal of the school was to push you to your maximum physical capability. The story we were told was the school was conceived from true survival stories of sailors in WWII. They found that elder sailors had a higher survival rate than their younger counterparts during times of high stress, such as while floating in the ocean on a piece of driftwood after your ship had been sunk. The elder sailors would often survive when the younger sailors didn't. Intuitively, one would think that youth would sustain a sailor longer. Apparently, however, the more mature sailors had the mental stamina to survive longer than the inexperienced youths. Outward Bound was conceived as a method of training people for survival by pushing them hard enough to find the true limits of their physical endurance. Indeed, during the month I spent at Outward Bound, I witnessed classmates finding their personal limits and breaking down. As for me, it was no picnic, but I am better person for having attended.

I arrived in Gunnison, Colorado in a bus full of city kids, middle class brats like me, and one or two guys from very rich families. The bus made its way off the pavement on to a dirt road, somewhere near Gunnison, and drove up a slope to a field pocked with small, two-man pup tents. This was Outward Bound base camp. We would be here overnight and not see it again for a month.

There were about forty guys, all teenagers, participating in the school. We were broken up into five groups. Each group had an instructor. At the end of some days we would pitch camp with one or more of the other groups, but most nights it was just the eight of us in my group. That afternoon I lingered, cautiously making friends with the guys who had been assigned to my group. There were nine of us total in my group, with the instructor. Some from as far away as New Jersey. One guy, Jim Sharkoff, lived in Colorado Springs.

Early the next morning, at dawn, we were abruptly woken up and ordered out of our tents. All of us in just underwear had to follow our instructor, in a near full sprint, along a narrow trail, over and under fallen logs, up and down steep terrain until we arrived at a mountain stream and a small pool just large enough and deep enough for us to jump into. And that's what we were told to do. Jump in. Jump in we did, and climbed out even faster. This was snowmelt water that was trickling down from the high snowfields, forming a small and very cold stream. I thought to myself, "So this is what the month is going to be like."

The rest of the day was taken up by the distribution of camping gear to each camper. They handed each of us an old army-issue backpack, canteen, ropes and carabiners, climbing helmets, a poncho, and some food. They sat us down in a circle and lectured us on what was expected of us.

The safety talk was punctuated with graphic stories of climbers whose skulls had been smashed by falling rocks. These tough instructors left nothing to the imagination, and they knew that many of us had come from the sixties' drug culture. After putting the fear of injury and death into our heads, the lecture turned to drugs. The instructor who was addressing the group said, "I'm not stupid. I know that some of you guys have dope on you right now." There was a stiff silence as everyone glanced around the circle and tried to appear innocent.

"We're gonna hand out plastic bags for you to put your dope in," the instructor said. "Leave your name on a piece of paper in the bag and we'll return the dope when you arrive back here in a month. And that includes any cigarettes. If you don't do as I say and we catch you with dope or cigarettes, you'll be kicked out and sent home." The danger of someone being high when your life was in his hands needed no further explanation. Also, it was going to be difficult enough to breathe up in the mountains without cigarettes, and anyone who smoked would slow everyone else down.

Oddly enough, almost everyone complied. I didn't have any contraband to relinquish, and I was amazed at the stash of drugs that miraculously appeared. The only one, as far as I know, who didn't follow orders was a punk from New Jersey who refused to give up his cigarettes. He left that day on a bus back to Denver. From that moment on, we knew the instructors were serious. Later that day we were trucked to the trailhead where we set up our first camp.

After every five or six days of hiking, our food provisions would be resupplied. There are only so many days of food one can carry. We were also hauling heavy coils of rope, full canteens, cooking equipment, tents, and the like. At least once we dropped down in altitude from the high mountains and met a jeep that had been driven into the wilderness range as far as it could go along a muddy dirt road. The jeep brought us more dehydrated foods like macaroni and cheese, powdered mashed potatoes, and other just-add-water-and-boil foods you could find in any grocery store. We also had plenty of surplus military rations in small tin cans. We'd place the sealed cans in boiling water for a few minutes to heat up the contents and then open them with the can opener blade on a jack knife. We'd have races to see who could open a can the fastest. Once opened, no one raced to eat the canned food. It was palatable, but only because we were hungry.

The month-long survival school was broken up into four or five expeditions. Each expedition was limited in duration by how much food we could carry. We had very heavy backpacks, and trudged through hundreds of miles of incredibly difficult terrain. It rained and hailed for at least a few hours every single day for the entire time I was there. All along we were being evaluated on our performance, unbeknownst to us, by the instructors.

The instructors were an eclectic bunch. The leader of my group was Bill Repret. Bill was of slim build, about five-eight with dark brown hair. His hearing was not good. If you wanted to be heard, you'd have to address him loudly. A few years before, Bill had been in a soldier in Vietnam. A bomb had exploded close enough to him to permanently damage his hearing. "What was more scary," he said, "was that the bombs sucked up all the oxygen in the immediate area and you felt like you were going to suffocate."

Most of the other instructors were British. They collectively belonged to the Rock and Ice Club, a club of world-class mountain climbers. One of the Brits showed us pictures of a first ascent he had made on a peak in the Andes, and he wasn't the only one among them with a first ascent to his name. These guys were as tough as their steel-tipped ice picks.

At Outward Bound, a typical day was up at dawn, breakfast, and a long trek through incredibly rugged mountains in the San Juan range. We were often at or above the tree line, which was around twelve thousand feet above sea level. Each morning, to get going as quickly as possible, we assigned tasks. One or two people would make a fire and start to cook breakfast. Someone would fold up all the tarps that we used as tents. Someone else would squeeze the residual farts out of the sleeping bags and cram them tightly into nylon stuff bags. We always tried to camp near a stream, and some person would refill the canteens and add halazone tablets to purify the water. As soon as breakfast was served, someone would carry water from a stream to douse the fire, clean the campground and make the area appear as undisturbed as possible, out of respect for our surroundings.

Each expedition was a little more difficult than the one before it: more technical terrain, more miles per day, and less reliance on our instructor. It became our responsibility to orient ourselves with compasses and maps. If we were not careful, a wrong turn could result in being off course by tens of miles by the end of a day, and heated arguments arose over map interpretations. That same summer there had been fatalities at another Outward Bound school as a result of students who had not followed procedures correctly.

With only a few days left of the thirty at Outward Bound, the groups were broken up and reassigned for the final expedition. We were matched up, according to our physical strength and survival skills, with similarly rated campers from other groups. The instructors had convened the night before to compare notes on the students and rated their abilities. Each of us was reorganized to form a new group and given a map and an assignment. After reassignment, it became obvious to us how they had rated each group; those who had showed mental or physical weakness, those who had broken down and cried after a hellish day of mountaineering, and those who would not, could not, take their turn at carrying the heavy coils of rope on top of the very heavy backpacks, were given less demanding assignments. I was proud to know that I was assigned to the most skilled group of guys. However, it was a mixed blessing, as we were given the most difficult assignment.

For the next three days we were on our own—no instructor, no way to communicate to the outside world. Just a map, compass, and assignment. From where we started the trek, we had to be where the X on the map indicated in three days or fewer. For my group it was fifty miles through rugged terrain, crossing over high peaks and navigating razor-edge traverses between peaks, on trails where a slip could result in a fatal fall, or where a wrong turn could get us lost for days. We were given this assignment because our instructors had confidence in us, and satisfaction that they had prepared us as best they could.

There was one more challenge lurking. Each camper had to survive alone at near tree-line altitude for four days and three nights. All we had with us were the clothes we were wearing, a canteen, and a handful of matches. We also had a rain poncho, but no food or sleeping bag. After many days of difficult hiking, complete with sweat, pounding hearts, blistered feet, mud-caked legs, and high-altitude air sucking, I was looking forward to four days of relaxation. Those four days didn't turn out to be as regenerating as I had hoped they'd be. In fact, they were the hardest part of the trip.

We were each left alone, strung out a few miles apart from one another, on the side of a mountain. I was deposited among the Ponderosa pines on a difficult slope near a small stream. Among the moss covered boulders I found a place to call home. It was a pocket surrounded on three sides by boulders; a space large enough to sleep in. I stretched my poncho over the top to create a roof against the rain and hail. Nighttime approached freezing temperatures, and I spent most of the first day gathering firewood. I wanted to amass a fuel supply substantial enough to keep a fire burning all night long. The first night was damn cold. At one end of my shelter I kept a fire going. I'd slip off into sleep when I was warmed by the fire and then wake up shivering when the fire had died down. This cycle repeated itself all night, every night.

My days were occupied by finding more firewood. My energy level was very low. I was always cold. No food, and the lack of oxygen at this altitude, made it hard to keep up a steady pace of collecting firewood. Any fat reserves I may have had on my body had evaporated during the days of hard hiking. Hunger was a chronic distraction. One afternoon I walked to the other side of the stream, hopping from stone to stone, to a small meadow between the tall trees and searched the grassy area for anything edible. During an hour of searching I found two wild strawberries. When I crossed back over the stream I was still exhausted, hungry, and cold. The two strawberries I ate weren't worth the effort it took to find them.

The third night was very difficult. Still hungry and cold, I began to question my sanity. As I stoked the fire I said to myself, "What was I thinking to suggest to my parents that they send me to this hellish place?" It was a repeat of the two previous nights. Shivering with cold, I'd wake up and throw some branches on the fire. Sometime far into the night, I woke up and tossed a pine sprig on the glowing coals. It was laden with pine needles. It was getting harder to find dry wood, so I had no choice but to break off some low branches that weren't dead and dry. The branch didn't catch fire right away. It sat on top of the coals for a few minutes building up a cloud of dense white smoke trailing up toward the sky. After a short while the hot coals dried the branch and it burst into flames with a loud whoosh. Something nearby, some large animal, was frightened by the sound. Being not more than a few yards away, it got up and ran, crashing through the underbrush. I could hear its feet pounding the ground as it fled. It gave me a rush of adrenaline that kept me awake for the rest of the night.

The next day would be the last day of the solo expedition, and I was actually looking forward to hiking again.

Yet it was with my stories of mountaineering that I convinced Lewis that I knew my way around the San Juan Range in southwestern Colorado. He was always up for a good adventure, so it didn't take much effort from me to convince him that we'd have fun.

We had known each other for many childhood years. We rode the same yellow school bus each day to and from school. Lewis lived over the top of the hill and past the dairy farm. My family lived on the side of the hill, near where the land flattened out at the bottom and where the water ran off into a wooded swamp. There were rows of stone walls carving up the meadows on the side of the hill.

The top of the hill was bisected with a country road lined on both sides with nice middle class houses; the wealthy houses were at the far end. Strings of tall hardwood trees shaded the stone walls with long shadows over the meadow grasses and grazing cows.

On this eve of departure, I found my mind wandering to odd places. As a boy, I had a paper route along the road at the top of the hill. One of my customers was an old lady who reminded me of my grandmother. The way she dressed in clothes of a long ago era, and kept her hair close to her head under a net. Her house was probably the largest in the neighborhood and it seemed strange to me, a small boy, that she lived alone in such a large house. I liked her driveway, though—it was asphalt, and she had it painted green.

As a paperboy I knew the name of every customer on my route. Her name was Mrs. Wellman. She and her mother were survivors of the sinking of the *Titanic*. When she passed away at eighty years old on November 25, 1975 the *New York Times* wrote a small passage about her. "When Mrs. Wellman was 16 and studying in Paris, her father booked passage for her and her mother on the White Star line ship. They were to attend Dartmouth

College graduation ... 'I was just dozing off when I felt a jarring crash,' said Wellman later." But it was one quote in particular that would capture something of an ideal for me—something I strove for on that trip to Colorado. She said, "I particularly recall the British seamen were magnificent. They knew, of course, that they would lose their lives, but they calmly and carefully doled out blankets and biscuits to us as we got into a lifeboat."

I'm sorry to say that I never asked her about her adventure on the open seas. A missed opportunity. Frankly, as a child, I was intimidated by her old lady presence and the spooky resemblance to my father's mother—and Lewis and I were more interested in sneaking out at night and finding adventures of our own. As we got older, our ideas of what made a good adventure had grown along with us. And so, it didn't take much convincing to get Lewis to join me on a new journey in Colorado.

With everything loaded and ready to go, we drove to a friend's house after dinner to attend a party. With his parents away, he had invited some friends over to imbibe in the spirits—libations of beer, Boones Farm apple wine, and some smoking herbs. While the party was by no means in our honor, we figured that such a momentous occasion as our departure deserved at least *some* recognition by our peers. But seventeen and eighteen year olds, being what they were, were more concerned with their lives than ours, and we didn't get the big sendoff we had hoped for. A couple friends wished us well, and Lewis and I got into the car to begin the journey.

We figured we'd drive well into the night to get a good start on the first leg of the journey. The air was still hot and humid from the fading summer evening. The sky was clear and dotted by bright stars and planets. Having said our goodbyes, we started up the Rambler and headed down South Main Street in Topsfield. Our spirits were high, and with our adrenaline pumping we were going to drive all night and through the next day, nonstop until we reached Lewis's mom's apartment in downtown Chicago. Chicago was about 850 miles ahead of us—not that far, by our adventurous reckoning. We were on our way.

CHAPTER 3

The Bumblebee needed new shock absorbers, so every bump and pothole caused the car to rock up and down like a boat in rough seas. Clunking noises from under the car were commonplace. But after a few short miles from home, the noise turned into a grinding sound. As the sound began to crescendo, the car slowed at the same rate as the grinding noise increased. Applying more gas made the noise louder, and the car just coasted to a full stop.

Lewis and I just looked at each other. We were close enough friends to know what the other was thinking. What just happened? The car had died. Maybe it was a blessing in disguise. Better here than in the middle of nowhere. Now what?

We were still on South Main Street in Topsfield. There were no cell phones in those days, so we walked back to down town where there was a pay phone. There was a trick I knew to make free calls on a pay phone. Well, almost free. I knew how to use a penny in place of a dime, but it had to be one of the three-slot payphones. There were three holes in a row at the top of the phone in which to insert coins. From left to right, the slots were sized to accept a quarter, a dime, and a nickel. This type of phone also had the rotary dialer, no push buttons.

I walked into the snack shop across the street and bought a soft drink, which justified my taking a paper straw. I flattened the straw by grasping one end and pulling the straw between two fingers of my other hand. The next step was to insert the flat straw down though the dime slot, and slightly angled toward the right. By dropping a penny into the nickel hole, the hole farthest to the right, the bell would sound and you'd have a dial tone and could dial a local call. The straw somehow deflected the penny in such a manner that the phone mechanism recognized it as a dime.

If you wanted to make a long distance call, you'd need the assistance of an operator. You could reach her (male operators were rare, or nonexistent) by dialing zero. You'd tell her the number you wished to reach and she'd tell you how much money to deposit in the coin slots. With the straw still in place, you'd just keep adding pennies until the operator was satisfied with the amount. One penny was counted as ten cents. This little trick came in handy many a time, though I'm sure Ma Bell didn't appreciate it.

After a few calls, we located a towing company. Then we walked back to the Bumblebee, which sat about a mile and a half away, alongside the road. We discussed our options. We had just left a few of our friends in awe over our plans. Some were impressed with our courage, but there were a few skeptics who thought we were crazy. We weren't going to let our pride suffer at the hands of doubters. The damned Rambler was not going to dash our plans. As we waited for the tow truck to arrive we decided on Plan B: We'd hitchhike our way to Colorado. And back.

The station wagon was towed back to Lewis' grandmother's house. Lewis used his grandmother's car to give me a ride back home. My parents were surprised to see me, as they had expected me to be on the road by now. As I arrived at the front door, my mother stood in the doorway.

A screen door between us, she asked, "What happened?"

My mom was a stay-at-home mom. Standard fare for most middle class families of the time. I had an older brother in college, a younger sister in high school, and a younger brother in grammar school. She had her hands full. My father worked in sales management.

Being midsummer, my siblings were not in school. They were sitting at the breakfast table, eavesdropping as my parents and I discussed the plan. My family mostly listened and didn't say much. At eighteen, I knew better than any parent. I was totally indestructible and would have defied them if they tried to veto my objective. It came as somewhat of a surprise that no one at the breakfast table opposed our Plan B.

Dad asked, "Do you have enough money?"

"I think so," I said, which was satisfactory for him.

Mom asked, "How long will you be gone?"

Their questions relieved my tension and I felt my defenses lowering. Dad said, "Have a good time," and he headed off to work. Mom's only comment was an admonition to call home when we got there.

Strangely, I began to fear that I was actually going to begin hitchhiking two thousand miles in a few hours. Something inside me thought that my parents would stop me. Between the dead Rambler and my parents, my friends would have understood why our plans were thwarted. But they'd have given me a hard time about it, anyway.

As a child my bicycle was my prime mode of transportation. Mom was often too busy to ferry me around in the car. If my destination was within ten miles or so, she would tell me to ride my bike. Topsfield's landscape is not friendly to someone using pedal power— the town is just one hill after another, after another. There was one hill, Weaton's Hill, the very thought of which would make my heart beat faster and beads of sweat form on my forehead. When I grew a little older, as a young teenager, I learned how much easier it was to just stand on the side of the road facing traffic and point my thumb in the air, aiming it in the general direction of my travel. For shorter distances, a bicycle usually trumped "thumbing," but for more ambitions distances, hitchhiking became a standard mode of travel.

In those days, thumbing was a common and an accepted practice. Not every family had two cars and it was unusual for a teenager to have a vehicle. Hitchhikers were ubiquitous and nonthreatening. I was about to extend my hitch hiking range to two thousand miles. Lewis was no stranger to hitchhiking, either. That spring he had hitchhiked from East Lansing, Michigan, to Daytona Beach, Florida and back in less than a week—with a girl, no less. So we figured, why not? And think of all the gas money we'd save! Back then gas was only thirty cents a gallon, but still it'd be cheaper to hitch.

The next morning was a Saturday. I tested my thumbing acumen by using it to reach Lewis's grandma's house. The Rambler station wagon was where the tow truck driver had left it—in the driveway, still stuffed halfway up the back windows with camping gear. Our backpacks were somewhere in there and had to be located. We found them under the sleeping bags and camp stove. Holding my backpack in one hand and mentally measuring the volume of the supplies we had accumulated, it was obvious that much of what we wanted to bring would have to be left behind.

It was midmorning and the sun was already beaming down and a breeze was churning the dry soil into a small wisps of dust. Lewis had on a pair of worn-out blue jeans. With his dirty T-shirt and tangled hair, he didn't look like someone even I would give a ride to. I probably didn't look much better, but at least my pants weren't full of holes.

We crammed as much as we could into our backpacks—shirts, underwear, a few pair of socks, some snacks, gum, candy bars, and the like. We strapped our sleeping bags to the top of our packs. For a tent, we had a sheet of international-orange plastic tarp, eight feet by ten feet, that I folded up into a foot square with about three inches of loft. It went in the pack among my clothes. For pots and pans, we had taken a large coffee can and bent a coat hanger through two holes opposite each other along the top rim. The coat hanger served a double purpose as handle and a hanger. We each had one can hanging and clanging off the bottom of our packs. In my pack, I also had a fishing rod in two sections. Even when taken apart, though, it protruded about fifteen inches or so. Since we'd be doing a lot of walking, I brought along some Doctor Scholl's moleskin. It's an adhesive-backed, felt-like material that I had used in past hiking adventures. You place it over a blister to mitigate the friction of your skin rubbing against the inside of your footwear. It might come in handy, and it was the only luxury we allowed ourselves.

Packs full, we hefted them on our backs. Slightly bent over from the weight, we walked down the driveway and began the first leg of the excursion. After a short time, a neighbor stopped for us. We threw our packs in the trunk and we were off. Not far, though. He drove us a few miles and left us at the intersection of US Route 1 and Route 62 in Danvers, Massachusetts.

Our 2,350-mile journey to the Rockies was underway.

There was a store on one corner, Putnam Pantry, and Sullivan's Garage on the opposite side. Behind Putman Pantry was the ominous looking Danvers State Hospital, an insane asylum locally known as the Danvers nuthouse. It was perched on top of a hill and looked like a medieval castle—the type that nightmares are made of.

A few years earlier, as a fifteen year old, I had spent a summer working as a kitchen boy there. I had always managed to find a summer job since the age of twelve. I would make my way up US Route 1, asking for work at each business along the way until someone offered me a job. I had been fortunate enough, the summer of my fifteenth birthday, to have stopped into the hospital the day after some kitchen help had been fired. The newly unemployed miscreants had been doing something they shouldn't have and started a kitchen fire, so my first day on the job was cleaning white powder from the tops of every oven and air duct in the kitchen. The powder had been deployed from fire extinguishers.

As a fifteen year old, working in a mental institution was an eye opener—a close look at the daily life of humans with severe mental disorders. My day started at 5:30 a.m. to work the breakfast and lunch shifts. It was my job to deliver heavy stainless steel food carts to each ward. The carts were on four wheels and almost as tall as I was, but much heavier. Hot food, tea, and soups were placed in removable containers within the carts. It was also my job to make the tea: one hundred and twenty gallons at a time with a tea bag the size of a small duffel bag.

There was a network of tunnels below the hospital. Elevators from the wards would drop down to the tunnels. I pushed the food carts, loaded with hot food, into an elevator in the kitchen and down to the tunnels. Some of the patients were trusted to walk unsupervised within the walls of the hospital, too. The hospital staff encouraged me to use any willing patient to help me push the heavy carts. It usually cost me fifty cents, but was well worth it. The food carts where heavy and the tunnels were not all level.

Pushing a few hundred pounds of food uphill was work. I—we—would push them through the tunnels and up elevators to the designated ward where I'd leave the cart with a ward attendant.

At first, I was shocked to see adults who wore diapers and drooled. Some had the mental capacity of an infant. In one ward, I'd see the same gentleman standing in the same spot week after week against the wall carrying on a conversation with empty space. One younger man would tell me every day that he was being discharged the next day, and was going to his sister's house. Some patients were lucid enough that at first I wondered why they were committed to the hospital; Josh, one of the patients I knew by name, introduced himself when we met and told me about his family. He seemed normal to me until he introduced himself again and told me the exact same story, and introduced himself again and then started over again with the same story.

It was in the shadow of the nuthouse that Lewis and I found our second ride. Two guys heading to New York City stopped and let us in. After about ten miles heading south on Route 1 we turned onto Route 128 heading southwest. In about twenty-five miles, the Massachusetts

Turnpike intersected 128. So far so good. The weather was nice and traffic was light.

I asked Lewis how far he thought we might travel that day.

"Western New York or Ohio," he guessed.

Listening to the radio and watching the guardrail zip past us, light conversation and daydreaming consumed an hour or so until we reached the intersection of Route 86, about halfway across the state. This was the cutoff to New York City through Hartford, Connecticut. There was no tollbooth there— the highway just split in two. Our driver slowed the car and pulled onto the grass at the side of the highway a few hundred yards before his exit ramp. Lewis and I grabbed our packs and slid out of the back seat onto the grass shoulder. We had no choice but to walk alongside the Massachusetts turnpike, fully aware that pedestrians were not allowed.

So we walked, thumbs protruding until we were on the downside of a hill. As a car approached us from the turn over the hill, there was barely enough time for a driver to see us, size us up, and decide whether or not to pull over and stop—a poor spot to hitchhike. There were ways to increase the odds of getting a ride, and we wanted to make it as easy as possible for someone to give us a ride; I was convinced that Lewis' ragged blue jeans, with the holes all over them, might have cost us, but I kept my mouth shut because I knew it was too late to ask him to find another pair.

Before we walked a quarter of a mile, a blue and gray Massachusetts state police car screeched to a stop beside us. Lewis murmured, "Oh, shit."

The state trooper exited his car holding a pump shotgun in his left hand, pointed toward the sky. Neither of us moved or said a word.

"Put your hands on the car, step back and spread your legs apart," he commanded. As Lewis and I complied we just looked at each other. As we were being patted down, Lewis was the first to speak. He was the master of the understatement.

"Is there something wrong, officer?"

"You're under arrest."

"What did we do?" Lewis shot back.

"It's against the law to hitchhike on the Mass Pike."

After the officer patted us down, apparently checking for weapons, he ordered us into the backseat of his cruiser. Between us and the officer was steel mesh. Once we were all settled in the cruiser, the state trooper asked sarcastically over his shoulder, "You boys wouldn't have any weed on you, you know, like grass?"

We both chimed in simultaneously, "No, sir."

Little did he know that we each had a small stash hidden in our underwear, probably the first place they would look if they chose to search us.

Lewis sought to divert him. "I've hitchhiked on this highway several times and state troopers would just pass me by."

As the officer pulled the cruiser off the shoulder and into traffic he said, "We're arresting everyone today who's not supposed to be on the turnpike. An officer was shot yesterday by someone he pulled over."

Lewis responded, "That's horrible. I hope the officer will be okay."

There was no response from up front. I don't know if he picked up on Lewis's obsequious tone. Lewis could sweet-talk his way out of a sticky mess, but I was afraid we were over our heads this time.

"Where are we going?" Lewis asked.

"To the state barracks."

"Can't you just take us off the highway and let us go?"

"Can't do it."

Nothing was said for few moments until the trooper said, "Where are you boys going?"

"We *were* going to go mountain climbing in Colorado." I couldn't keep the sarcasm out of my voice.

He answered, "That's a long way to hitchhike."

We agreed and told him about our plans to drive and how we ended up where we were.

The trooper was softening. We were just two young adventurers. The conversation drifted from the broken-down Rambler to automobile safety. The trooper told us how much he admired Ralph Nader. Nader came to prominence in 1965 with the publication of his book *Unsafe at Any Speed*, a critique of the safety record of American automobile manufacturers in general, and most famously the Chevrolet Corvair.

We approached a building close to the highway. A sign on the facade declared it as the Massachusetts Turnpike Authority. The police barracks. It may have been a station for highway maintenance machines and crew, as well, because some heavy machinery sat in the back parking lot behind a chain link fence.

The building was on the opposite side of the highway. The trooper pulled the car through a paved path in the median that had a sign that said *No Unauthorized Vehicles*. He crossed the traffic lane and entered the barracks parking lot. He told us to stay put and got out of the car. He headed inside the barracks.

Lewis looked at me, and in a slightly panicked voice, asked, "Should we hide the pot under the seat?"

"NO!"

The trooper came back outside and approached. In the back of my mind, I was wondering if hiding contraband in the car is exactly what the trooper wanted us to do, and was the reason he left us alone in the car. If we were caught, our new adventure would include arrest, court, jail, fines, and hell to pay with our parents, not to mention a criminal record. Little did we know that jail was already on the menu.

The trooper ordered us out of the car. We got out and grabbed our backpacks from the trunk of the vehicle, threw them over our shoulders, and were ushered inside. We were told where to sit. Once seated, we were asked to produce identification. Lewis and I pulled out our wallets and driver's licenses and handed them over. The desk officer asked us what were doing on the highway, so we repeated the story we had already told the arresting officer.

The room had a coffee machine on a table. The windows were barred, and there were a few other state troopers sipping coffee and looking at us as we recited our story. They were making small talk and throwing glances our way. They were intimidating and I did not want to create trouble for anyone. Lewis poured on his usual charm, no doubt trying to dissuade a body search.

The troopers didn't pay us much attention until I came to the part of the story about our intentions of going hiking in the Rocky Mountains. One of the troopers walked up, eyed my backpack and said, "I hope you guys make it." His statement took me by surprise. I was intimidated by these guys, and their friendliness was unexpected.

The trooper reached for the crushed Doctor Scholl's box that was sticking out of the top of my pack. "What's this?"

I explained that it was moleskin in case I got any blisters on my feet while hiking.

He responded, "That's great planning. Send us a postcard when you get there."

These guys were actually human. As one of two young longhairs, I was afraid that they'd take joy in kicking our asses. My tension subsided, but I was still worried about being searched.

After our vitals were taken by the desk officer, the arresting officer marched us back out to the car. It was early afternoon by now. Traffic was heavy. The sun was at its peak. I'm not sure if the sweat on my face was due to the summer heat or our predicament, but I was starting to believe we had just made a narrow escape.

Lewis asked, "Are you taking us someplace off the highway to drop us off?"

"You might say that."

We drove along some country roads and I hoped he wouldn't leave us somewhere too isolated, or else we'd never be able to hitch our next ride. I saw a sign indicating that we were headed towards Southbridge, Massachusetts, only a few minutes from the police barracks we had just left.

The police cruiser came to a stop in front of a brick building near downtown.

The trooper said, "This is your new home."

Lewis and I glanced and each other and shrugged. What did he mean by that?

It turned out to be the local jail. Inside was a man sitting behind a massive oak desk that looked more like a teller's booth at a bank. He was a big guy, and he glared at us without much expression on his face. It was our second oh-shit moment of the day.

The trooper addressed the man behind the desk. "I have some guests for you."

The man replied, "We have a couple of nice rooms for these two boys."

I'm thinking, *Holy shit, we are never going to make it to Colorado.* I don't know Lewis's exact thoughts, but they were probably on track with mine. Somehow we had to get out of this.

"Put your packs against that wall," the desk officer said, pointing to the wall opposite the desk, "and follow me." We marched single-file behind him through a large door into an adjacent room. Taking up the rear was the state trooper.

"Here is your new home," said the desk officer.

Lewis and I stood looking at a row of holding cells—heavy metal bars on all sides, barred doors open, ready to accept a new occupant.

"You each get a cell."

Lewis, being quick-witted, said, "Are you going to take our belts so we don't hang ourselves?"

The desk officer chucked and replied, "As a matter of fact, yes."

What lent this scene some humor was the fact that there was a popular song playing in the background—"Alice's Restaurant" by Arlo Guthrie. There was a short movie associated with the song that today would have been called a video. In the story, Arlo Guthrie is arrested for littering. He's put in jail where he has to surrender his belt so he wouldn't hang himself. It's a funny video. Ironically, it took place in western Massachusetts, somewhere very close to where we were at the very moment. The humor wasn't lost on any of us, and the desk officer gave up a laugh.

After removing our belts, we crossed the threshold into our new digs. The doors clanged shut behind us. I don't know if I was more amused or disappointed. I had never been behind bars before and Arlo Guthrie had written the script.

Lewis and I looked through the bars at each other. I said, "They'll never believe us when we get home."

Always thinking, Lewis called out to the desk officer as he was about to pass through the big door to the front room, "Sir? Can you take our pictures?" The officer slowed his pace. "There's a camera in the side pocket of the green backpack."

A few moments later he reappeared with Lewis's 35 mm single-lens reflex camera. Lewis showed him which button to push. The officer stepped back a few paces and focused the camera on Lewis's cell. Lewis posed with his face framed between two bars, his hands at about the height of his ears. He had a shit-eating grin on his face. I heard the shutter click. The officer advanced the film with his thumb by swinging a lever on the side of the camera. I struck the same pose as Lewis.

"You boys are all right," the officer said, and retreated to his desk.

The state trooper was long gone by now. The reality of our situation was beginning to set in.

Lewis yelled though the bars, "How long are we gong to be here?"

"You can get released when each one of you pay a $15 fine."

His answer came as a relief. Okay, I thought, let's just pay and leave. But before the thought had finished coalescing in my brain, the officer added, "The bailiff will be here Monday. You can pay him then."

We were in jail and it was Saturday. Damn! True to form, Lewis turned on his Eddie Haskel charm. If anyone could talk his way out of jail, Lewis could.

"Excuse me, sir. Fifteen dollars for two nights room and board in this beautiful town is a real bargain." Geez, Lewis, I was thinking to myself, sarcasm may not be a wise move. To my relief I heard the officer chuckle as he passed through the door into the cell area. He stood outside of our cells, bars between us and him. Lewis continued, "We shouldn't be wasting the taxpayers' money. Can't we just pay you, and then you can pay the bailiff on Monday?"

The officer pondered for a moment. "I can't do that, but let me see what I can do for you boys. I'll call the bailiff at home and see if he'll come over." He disappeared through the door into the other room. We could hear the rotary phone dialing. We heard bits and pieces of the conversation that followed. I heard "good boys" and "hitchhiking" in between a few chuckles. The officer wandered back into the cell area and announced that the bailiff would come by to take our fines when he finished mowing his lawn.

Lewis, with his blue jeans that appeared to have been eaten by moths, might have kept people from stopping their cars to give us a ride, but his contribution as the consummate bullshitter had saved the day.

A few hours later the bailiff arrived.

Lewis opened up with a full volley of charm. "Thank you, sir, for taking your personal time today to take our fines and release us."

The bailiff just stood and stared at Lewis. After taking a good look at us, I think he was having second thoughts. Once again, his jeans were not helping.

The officer had a key in his hand and opened my cell door. I stepped out and he moved a few steps sideways to Lewis's cell door. He had some trouble inserting the key into the lock. He wiggled the key up and down and sideways but managed to push it in with the weight of his body. He rattled the bars in the door as he did so.

The bailiff stood behind the officer and looked over his shoulder as he struggled to turn the key. The lock was jammed.

"Let me try," said the bailiff.

The smirk on Lewis' face was fading into a look of concern. Both men tried a few times to turn the key. They were both becoming frustrated and their demeanor erased any thought I had that they were just playing a mean trick.

After a few anxious moments, the bailiff managed to release the lock. The decrepit mechanism would not, after all, sentence Lewis to an undetermined stint behind bars. Lewis and I were out. We thanked the bailiff and officer, who said, "Good luck, boys, send a postcard when you get to Colorado."

Lewis and I stepped outdoors with our packs on our backs, our long hair, and Lewis' shredded blue jeans. The state trooper was long gone. He was our only hope for a ride back to the highway. Fat chance that he'd agree to give us a ride back to the highway, anyway. We knew the general direction back to the turnpike, so we stood on the side of the road, faced traffic, and stuck our thumbs out. We were in rural Massachusetts just outside of Southbridge. The street was lined with tall maple trees in full bloom. A sidewalk meandered though the giant trees. There was a soft breeze rustling the leaves, mitigating the wrath of the afternoon sun. But there weren't any cars.

After a while, a pickup truck came to a stop beside us. The driver said, "Throw your packs in the back."

We did as he said and both of us climbed into the front seat of the truck. It had a single bench seat and a shift rod sticking up from the floor. I sat in the middle and had to lean to get out of the way every time the man shifted gears.

The Massachusetts Turnpike was only a few miles away. We were dropped off, again, at an entrance ramp. We had learned our lesson, the hard way, to not hitchhike on the highway itself. The entrance ramps were the place to be. It turned out that we weren't the only travelers who had learned that rule. Strung out in front of us were several other hitchhikers, all trying to attract a ride. There was one group of four, and a couple of duos. The person first in line, a guy about our age, was hitchhiking with his dog. There seemed to be an unwritten rule, a common courtesy, that it was first-come, first-served. Lewis's jeans may have been a deterrent to forward progress, but a dog might slow us down even more.

Lewis and I waited patiently for our turn. While we waited, we ate some candy bars and sat on our backpacks behind a green traffic sign. There had been no food in jail. A Snickers bar and a box of raisins took care of my immediate needs. Traffic was heavy and slow, and the air beside the pavement was sweltering. A car pulled up next to us and a gal rolled down the window and handed Lewis a half-full cup of Coke—and kept driving.

My eyes were drawn to the back of the street sign. Someone had written a message. Upon closer inspection, there were in fact many short messages on the back of the sign. *Still waiting for a ride after two hours*, was one. Not very encouraging. There were a few handwritten names and dates.

I noticed that the lead hitchhiker, the one at the head of the pack, had turned down a ride from a car that had pulled over. He and his dog were about fifty yards from us along the pavement so we couldn't hear their conversation. It dawned on me that the entrance ramp to the turnpike was shared by both eastbound and westbound traffic. Not far from where we waited, I found a piece of cardboard.

Among our camping supplies Lewis found a pencil, so I used it to write WEST. I figured that this might expedite the process when Lewis and I became the lead hitchhikers.

It was a good idea, but it didn't hurry the line along. We kept waiting. Our time would come.

There weren't many hours of daylight left when Lewis and I took over the coveted lead hitchhiking spot. By now there were several travelers who had entered the queue behind us. They were patiently waiting their turn, like us, fervently hoping we would be picked up.

The WEST sign did its trick. It wasn't more than a few minutes until we were offered ride. A blue-gray VW Beetle stopped and the passenger asked where we going. Lewis responded, "Colorado."

The driver said, "Climb in."

Climb in was the appropriate phrase. There were two people in front and one in back. It was an acrobatic feat to climb into the rear seat with my big backpack, and even harder for Lewis, who was taller than I. Still, a ride was a ride, and we were happy to finally be on the road again.

NO SHIRT, NO SHOES, NO SERVICE

But sitting on the hump in the middle of the backseat with a heavy pack in my lap, blocking my forward view, was uncomfortable. My fishing pole was sticking up through the top of my pack and had to be removed so it wouldn't puncture the roof liner. I felt bad for the guy on my left. Before we had entered the scene, he had the whole backseat to himself. Now he just had a window.

We drove along the Mohawk River seeing signs for Albany, New York. VW Beetles had no air conditioning, so the breeze from the open windows was the only relief. The sun was starting to go down and it would be dark at about the time we reached our hosts' destination.

"Okay, guys, this is where we get off," the driver said as he tilted his head back toward me. We were at the outskirts of Albany on Route 90, the New York State Throughway. The driver pulled the VW Bug to the side of the road after he had paid the toll taker. It was night, but the road was lit up with street lamps.

The toll station serviced the traffic exiting the highway as well as the entering vehicles. Lewis and I thanked the driver and walked across the asphalt to the side where traffic was entering the westbound side of the turnpike. There we stood with our WEST sign and waited for a ride.

As we stood, we recounted the day's experiences. We were disappointed that we had only made it to Albany. If we hadn't been arrested and put in jail, we might have been somewhere in Ohio. Instead we had only traveled about 250 miles. The broken-down Rambler, the day behind bars ... Had these incidents been an omen?

There wasn't much traffic. The streetlights cast long shadows in several directions. Because it was nighttime, drivers had less time to look us over and make a judgment about our amity. To me, Lewis still resembled a scarecrow with his torn jeans. Drivers let caution rule their decisions and no one stopped to pick us up. It had been a long day. We were tired. The adrenaline of the adventure's first day had worn off. We took a few steps down the embankment, out of sight from travelers and tollbooth attendants, and rolled out our sleeping bags.

CHAPTER 4

Sunday, we woke to the sound of traffic. The sun had just come over the horizon. The sky was clear of clouds and the weather still appeared to be on our side. There was a truck stop about a mile beyond the tollbooth, away from the highway, and we were hungry.

With our packs slung over our shoulders we trudged along the side of the road, kicking up a low cloud of dust as we headed for the truck stop. There was a large parking lot with a dozen or so big rigs parked between the herringbone-patterned lines on the pavement. The big diesel engines chugged, idling. The smell of diesel exhaust permeated the air. There wasn't even a slight breeze, and the dew hadn't yet evaporated from the windshields of the automobiles parked among the trucks.

At the other side of the parking lot was a cafe. It was a single-story building with large glass windows facing the parking lot. Inside were a few rows of booths beside the windows. In the back of the restaurant was a serving counter with bar stools and some tables scattered haphazardly in the open space. A young waitress worked behind the counter and a cook whose back was to us.

A smattering of hungry truckers ate their breakfasts, and no one paid much attention to us. A greasy spoon like this had probably fed all types of travelers. Lewis and I chose a booth and sat down. It was a good place to stow our backpacks, and the view through the window was better than the view inside.

A waitress sauntered over and took our order. After we ate our fill we walked back the quarter mile past the tollbooth and parked ourselves on the westbound ramp. The sun was beginning to beat down and it was going to be another hot August day. We had barely gone two hundred miles the first day, and still had four times that distance to get to Chicago. Our timetable was shot to pieces and we wondered if we'd ever reach the mountains.

Sunday was a long day of waiting at tollbooths for the occasional short-hop ride. In fits and starts we made it across New York and into Ohio. Mid-afternoon, we got picked up by a friendly guy near Cleveland; unfortunately,

NO SHIRT, NO SHOES, NO SERVICE

I left my fishing pole in his backseat. So much for fishing in the alpine lakes. Closer to dusk, a young couple a few years older than us, pulled over in a station wagon and offered us a ride. They were heading west on Route 90, but not very far. They were involved with 4H and going to the county fair where they planned to set up the 4H booth in a pavilion on the fairgrounds.

Lewis and I were no stranger to county fairs. Topsfield boasted the oldest continuous county fair in the United States. As kids, we knew every way there was to sneak onto the fairgrounds without paying the gate fee. Many of our friends would try to get a job with one of the carnival rides for the week long fair. The carnival crowd were a seedy bunch, though, and if you didn't keep an eye on your boss at the end of the week, they would often try to skip town without paying your wages.

The couple driving the station wagon had gate passes. They showed them at the gate and drove right onto the fair grounds with Lewis and I in the backseat. We had volunteered to help them set up the 4H booth, and in return, the couple offered to bring us back to the highway when the fair closed for the evening. After giving them a hand unloading the car and setting up the 4H booth we were free to wander around.

This county fair was small compared to the Topsfield Fair, but the theme was the same: agricultural displays, livestock barns, and a midway of carnival rides complete with a Ferris wheel, as well as assorted other mechanical contraptions for which people paid good money to end up dizzy and nauseated. There was a short alley lined by game booths where patrons would try their hand at beanbag tossing and throwing darts at balloons. Big stuffed animals hanging in the booths tricked people into thinking that they were winnable. It was no surprise that we saw no one win a big prize. It was the same con game here as it was at the fair back home. Someone lucky enough to throw a beanbag through the cardboard clown's mouth would be handed a pint-size doll. Then the carnival barker would try to capture the attention of the next sucker who was trying to impress his girlfriend.

Lewis and I were savvy to the crooked carnival games and we didn't have any extra cash that we could waste, anyway. We mostly just walked around looking at pretty Ohio girls. I had never been to any county fair other than the Topsfield Fair. This one was no different. A few minutes before closing time we wandered back to the pavilion and found our 4H friends. We helped them take down their booth and close it up for the night. They brought us back to the highway and dropped us of at the exit.

Lewis and I tried our luck and scored another ride right way, albeit a short one. We hopscotched further west with a few more short rides. The second-to-last ride of the night was a guy and two girls who said it would be okay to crash at their place if we wanted. We thought about it, then decided not to take them up on their offer.

The last ride was a station wagon with four guys about our age or maybe a year or two younger. Maybe still in high school. There was room for us and our gear, they didn't appear to be threatening, so we accepted the ride. After climbing in we exchanged the usual pleasantries. I sensed that these guys were a little intimated by strange hippies from the East Coast. Our hosts all had well groomed, short hair. They were T-shirted, trim, and athletic-looking—farm-born and -bred.

Small talk led to the story of how we had arrived where we were. By the time we explained our plan, they were looking at us as if we were Lewis and Clark instead of

Lewis and Steve. One of them blurted out, "We're going camping tonight, do you guys want to join us?"

I caught the concerned expression of his other buddy's face, and answered, "Sure," before any objections could be voiced. It was a done deal.

The driver swung the car off the pavement onto a dirt road. We followed the road a few hundred yards in the dark until he stopped in a sand pit. It was an open area a few acres wide with scatted piles of sand and stone. He pulled the car to a stop near a mound of sand. There were the remnants of a campfire encircled by stones. We all piled out of the car. Two of the guys walked off into the darkness and reappeared a few minutes later with armfuls of firewood. They had obviously been here before.

The night air was a cool and refreshing change from the hot fairgrounds. There were stars in the sky in between the wispy, high-altitude clouds. The moon shone through as the clouds passed, giving us enough light to get a glimpse of our surroundings. Before long the campfire was blazing and felt hot on my sunburned face. The beer broke out, and without needing to ask, I was handed a cool bottle of it.

It had been a long day and Lewis and I were ready to relax with the buzz of cannabis between our ears. Lewis approached the subject cautiously with our new friends.

"Do you guys have any pot?" he asked. I knew what Lewis was trying to do. If someone had responded with some pot-fearing vitriol, the plan would have been aborted and he'd change the topic of conversation.

Instead, one of them answered, "No, but I'd like to try it someday."

The others nodded their agreement. The coast was clear.

Lewis reached in his pocket, pulled out a small baggie containing the evil weed and handed it to the guy sitting next to him. It made its way around the circle as each of them took their first look. Lewis rolled a few thin cigarettes, lit them, and passed them around. Our new friends were likable guys—they were genuinely interested in us as we were anomalous to their daily reality. To them, we were worldly. We were adventurous. We had long hair. And now, we also had some marijuana.

In a few minutes I was asleep on top of my rolled-out sleeping bag.

When I woke up the next morning, the dew had covered the top layer of my sleeping bag, so I spread it open in the sun. Lewis was already up and about. One by one our friends came to life, stood up and stretched. The campfire had long since died out, but the smell of smoke still lingered in the air.

The gang of four dropped us of at an entrance ramp to the highway. We said our goodbyes and Lewis and I were on our way again, though exaggerated tales of our presence would probably circulate among that gang for years.

We started our Monday morning with a short hop, and then we finally got lucky. A guy in a yellow VW Beetle picked us up. Next to him in the car was a huge black dog. The guy had removed the passenger seat to make room for Fido, who might have been a Newfoundland. He constantly drooled and slobbered all over everything, and his wet-dog odor permeated the upholstery. The owner had a few old blankets on the floor for the dog to sit (and slobber) on.

The guy was pretty cool. He had long dark brown hair and a mustache. Lewis and I could see that he was very much like us. He had an easy manner and was easy to talk to. The conversation led one way and another, and after a while, we learned that he was a parole officer. He worked with a lot of men who'd spent time at Cook County Jail for relatively minor offenses. He asked us if we had any pot, which we did, so shared a little smoke with him and had a good ole trip into Chicago. As we rode along, he told us stories about his parolees and the notorious Cook County Jail. He cautioned that we *never* wanted to go there. He even took us right to the main entrance of Lake Point Tower, which was where Lewis's mother lived. It was early afternoon and we had finally finished the first leg of our journey, a day late and at least thirty dollars short.

Lake Point Tower is located beside Lake Michigan on East Grand River, right next to Navy Pier in the heart of the city. At seventy stories, it was the largest apartment-only building in the world at the time. Seen from the sky, it was shaped like a three-leaf clover. Almost every apartment had a fantastic view of the city.

Lewis' mother lived on the sixtieth floor. I couldn't wait to see the view from up there. She said she would leave a key to her apartment with the doorman, a big heavyset

African American. Lewis approached the doorman, who, by his big welcoming smile, was expecting to see us. But just to be sure we were who we said we were, the doorman asked Lewis what the apartment number was.

Lewis answered, "Six thousand and one."

The doorman let out a big laugh and said, "Boy, we ain't got six thousand floors here! You mean Sixty-Oh-One?" We learned the proper way to specify an apartment was the floor number, then the apartment number. So apartment 6001 was Sixty-Oh-One. Still laughing, he gave Lewis the key and we went on our way, glad to be here and happy that we had made the guy's day.

Walking through the lobby to the bank of elevators, we got quite a few stares. Long dirty hair, big backpacks with tin cans swinging and clanging as we walked. Lewis with his jeans that looked like they had been used for target practice. And not having showered, shaved or changed clothes since Saturday morning, we probably left a kaleidoscope of odors behind us. There were a lot of exclusive shops, restaurants, and hair salons on the first three floors, and most of the people there were well-heeled. After passing through a gauntlet of scrutiny we made it to the bank of elevators. I felt it was a victory that we made it that far without being asked to leave.

Now that we were here we realized we had to choose the correct elevator. There were several express elevators that only serviced certain ranges of floors. The one that serviced the penthouse floor required a special key. We found the one that serviced the sixtieth floor, stepped in and were whisked to our destination. The door opened, we looked left and then to the right, and there was apartment 6001.

The apartment itself was new and nice. The kitchen was small, but the appliances were modern and stylish. It had a big living room with a dining area to one side and a small utility room with washer, dryer, and half-bath. Through a door from the kitchen was a single bedroom with an attached bathroom. Nothing spectacular except the view.

Sixty stories up, the entire wall of the living room was a series of uninterrupted windows. Her apartment looked north—one third of the view over the Lake Michigan shore and the other two thirds over the city. We were looking through a canyon of tall buildings. The John Hancock building was the tallest in Chicago at the time, and dominated the panorama. And being on the sixtieth floor meant you could look down on most of Chicago. Little turquoise rectangles dotted the cityscape: I was surprised at how many buildings had rooftop pools.

Along the wall of windows was a seat that ran the length of the room. A pair of high-powered binoculars sat beside the windows on a pile of books.

We made ourselves lunch and did a load of laundry. Afterward we took a nap. Lewis's mom came home at about five thirty. She worked at the Chicago Merchandise Mart as a sales rep for Vincent Lippe Corp. Bob, her significant other and future husband, showed up a half hour later to have dinner with the three of us. Bob worked for Sears and was an assistant vice president of store planning.

Bob was a good-looking fellow with a personality that made us feel like we were already old friends. His wit was sharp and his intelligence obvious. He was physically fit, about six feet tall with carefully coiffed dark brown hair. After dinner we all played a game of gin rummy. (In between highway rides, sitting beside various roadways the previous two days, Lewis had taught me how to play. Playing cards helped kill the boredom while Lewis's pants, the ultimate ride repellent, were quietly at work.) Bob sat to my left during the game. I watched his play carefully and was cautious not to discard anything he'd find useful.

Soon, he asked me how long I had been playing gin rummy.

I answered, "In hours a few, in days only two."

He responded, "You play better than most people who have played for years."

I took that as a great compliment.

After dinner, Lewis asked his mother if we could borrow her car. He wanted to take me to Old Town. Lewis had been here before and wanted to show off the city to me. We changed into clean clothes—and clean they were, but Lewis actually wore his jeans. We took the elevator down to the subterranean parking garage. Down in the underground garage we found her 1968 silver Pontiac LeMans right where it was supposed to be. It was one of a matching pair of cars his parents had bought when they got divorced. It was still a decent car three years later. Upon leaving the garage in the LeMans we drove west on Grand River, north on LaSalle, and then west to Wells.

Old Town was the coolest part of Chicago back then. There were lots of bars, shops, and restaurants. Lots of people too, and cops—for good reason. Old Town was

Blackstone Ranger territory. At the time they were the biggest street gang in America with over fifty thousand members. Two cops looked at Lewis' jeans and one asked, "What happened to you, a bomb?"

A little later two black kids walked by and asked if we wanted to buy some dope. We said no, and a couple seconds later a third black kid walked by and said "F—k you."

We were approached a couple more times by other budding entrepreneurs. Lewis had a short discussion with a black kid and negotiated a purchase. He wanted to have plenty for the rest of the trip. I had one ear toward their conversation and an eye looking out for Chicago's finest. The young sales rep told Lewis to follow him down an alley toward a tenement. To me this smelled dangerous.

"Don't do it Lewis," I cautioned. I told him he was crazy and no way would I go with him. There are times when you have to follow your gut instincts, so I watched as Lewis and his "friend" disappeared through a door into the tenement building. I wondered if he'd ever come back alive.

Ten minutes later he reappeared. He'd gone with the guy to the lobby of a tenement building where they smoked a joint. Lewis wanted to sample the product before he made an investment. After Lewis's stamp of approval, the guy said, "Give me the money and I'll go upstairs and get the stuff." Lewis finally began to see that he was going to be ripped off and refused to give the kid the money. He had to get out of there. His "friend" began to get angry so Lewis gave him a couple of bucks for the joint he'd smoked and quickly retreated. He was lucky, in my opinion, and very naive.

We spent some more time in Old Town visiting record stores and head shops. At one shop Lewis replenished our supply of rolling papers. On the drive back to Lake Point Tower we drove south on LaSalle and took a spin on the Lower Wacker Drive. The road went *under* the city from near the lakeshore to the Eisenhower Expressway. The tunnel was decorated with horizontal, colored stripes that made it look like a rainbow. It was a favorite sight for visitors.

We made it back to the apartment building, parked the car in the underground garage, and took the high-speed elevator to Sixty-Oh-One and spent some time looking out over the city. The field glasses made all the difference in the world. With them you could see inside the nearest buildings, many of which had apartments. It's amazing how many people leave their curtains open. We could see a lot of people inside their offices and apartments through the windows. We weren't the only Peeping Toms; I spotted one guy looking over the city through a gigantic telescope. I waited to see if he would look our way so I could wave, but it didn't happen. It made me wonder what he saw that justified the expense of his telescope.

Pretty soon Lewis's mom reminded us she had to go to work tomorrow and we somewhat uncomfortably turned in. She said we could share her queen size bed and she would sleep on the couch. Sleeping with another guy in a bed, even a queen-sized one, just felt weird—we were close friends, but not that close.

Tuesday morning, Bob stopped by and picked us up on his way to the office. He took us to Interstate 80, south of the city, and dropped us off. He thought it incredulous that we just wanted to be let off at the on-ramp. We assured him we knew what we were doing. After all, we were experienced hitchhikers, and we were in our element again.

NO SHIRT, NO SHOES, NO SERVICE

Fortunately, I-80 was not a toll road in Illinois (nor Iowa, nor Nebraska, for that matter) and so we were confident that it would be okay to hitchhike from the bottom of the ramp. We rode a number of short hops and made it into Iowa by mid-afternoon. It was progress, but not great progress. Again we noticed that that there were messages and travelogues written on the backs of many of the highway signs. Some were no more than "Kilroy was here" notes with names and dates; others were autobiographical sketches, all by hitchhikers like us. We felt like we were part of some shadowy underground brotherhood that included not only hitchhikers but motorcyclists, as well. We felt the bikers were good guys, like us hitchhikers. It was understood that there was no way they could pick us up, and therefore no way they could turn us down, unlike everyone else on the road. Virtually every guy on a bike would give you the upraised fist of solidarity as he sped by. We answered in kind, mindful of the solemn responsibility we bore simply by being part of something larger than ourselves.

As minutes standing in the sun turned into hours, all the cars and trucks that passed us by were somehow the enemy. Sometimes our frustration came to the surface and we'd show them a personal digital communicator of our own. Big rig truckers never gave us a ride.

By this time I was getting irritated by Lewis' machine-gun-riddled jeans. I made him sit on the side of the road with his backpack in front of him to hide the holes. I was convinced he was scaring off potential rides.

Late in the afternoon our prayers were answered. A station wagon pulled over and stopped in front of us. We saw that it was crammed full of cargo and had a single male occupant. He asked where we going and we said Durango, Colorado. He smiled and said he was driving nonstop from New York to San Francisco. He said, "Get in," and we gladly obliged. So we stuffed our backpacks in the back, helped him carve out a space on the left side of the rear seat, and off we went.

He asked, "Are you guys willing to drive some?"

After waiting on the side of the highway as long as we had, we'd even be willing to push. Our new chauffeur was tired of driving so Lewis took the wheel. After a half hour of small talk, Lewis asked him how fast we could drive.

The guy answered, "I don't care. It's your ticket," and he promptly fell asleep. We didn't know who was happier to be together on our way west—him or us. The miles flew by as we raced off into the sinking sun.

As it turned out, we did almost all the driving. Our traveling companion was lawyer. He had a New York accent, which was much different from the Upstate one, and he explained that he was moving his residence from New York to California.

He said, "The FBI thinks that I have been defending too many political radicals. They've been watching me. I think they were tapping my phone." He went on to say that his roommate in college was Abbie Hoffman, the iconic leader of the countercultural underground youth movement of the sixties and seventies. He was a war protester, and in the eyes of the authorities, a general rabble-rouser. Hoffman had been arrested and tried for conspiracy and inciting to riot as a result of his role in anti-Vietnam War protests, which were met by a violent police response during the 1968 Democratic National Convention in Chicago. He was among the group that came to be known as the Chicago Seven (originally known as the Chicago Eight), which included fellow Yippie Jerry Rubin, David Dellinger, Rennie Davis, John Froines, Lee Weiner, future California state senator

Tom Hayden and Black Panther Party cofounder Bobby Seale. On February 18, 1970, Hoffman and four of the other defendants (Rubin, Dellinger, Davis, and Hayden) were found guilty of intent to incite a riot while crossing state lines. All seven defendants were found not guilty of conspiracy. At sentencing, Hoffman suggested the judge try LSD and offered to set him up with "a dealer he knew in Florida" (the judge was known to be headed to Florida for a post-trial vacation). Each of the five was sentenced to five years in prison and a $5,000 fine. In 1971, Hoffman published *Steal This Book*, which advised readers on how to live basically for free. Many of his readers followed Hoffman's advice and stole the book, leading many bookstores to refuse to carry it.

A few hours passed as we drove though Iowa and into Nebraska. We Easterners know Iowa and Nebraska to be among those "big square states"—approximately six hundred and fifty miles of highway through the two of them. For all practical purposes, they seemed like a single state. Neither have any geographical differences that distinguish one from the other. It was about the flattest place on earth I had ever seen. There always seemed to be a single tree in the distance. Thirty minutes later it was *still* in the distance. Between towns, there were cornfields from one horizon to the other and absolutely nothing else except that one tree and an occasional grain silo. You would often see a dirt road running perpendicular to the highway, bisecting a cornfield. We couldn't see where they led to but were probably a driveway or a tractor path to corn heaven. There were very few houses.

Once we were in Nebraska, traffic was light, mostly big trucks that went by at insanely high speeds. Lewis and I took turns at the wheel, stopping only for gas and a bite to eat. The guy in back only got out once to go to the bathroom and that was it. By the time night came we were barreling along at over ninety miles per hour and basically just keeping up with the sparse traffic. We zoomed past a Nebraska State Police cruiser on the side of the highway at almost a hundred miles an hour and it didn't seem to faze him a bit. At least he didn't bother to chase us down. The miles melted away and we began to see signs for Julesburg, Colorado, and Interstate 76.

We had come to the end of our time in Nebraska and it was time to head southwest for Denver. Our travel companion tried to talk us into going all the way to San Francisco with him. We had made his trip a lot easier and he didn't want to give us up quite yet. I have to admit, I considered ditching the mountain climbing plans to see the West Coast. I had never been there, and in front of us was the opportunity. I vacillated, and I think Lewis might have done the same, but in the end we made the right decision. We got out of the car.

Still in Nebraska, and at the northeast corner of Colorado (another one of those big square states), we pulled over where Interstate 76 heads southwest toward Denver and Interstate 80 continues west toward San Francisco. It was nighttime when we gathered our packs from the back of the car and stood on the side of the road next to the endless cornfield. We thanked our friend for the ride, and in turn he thanked us for taking the wheel and letting him get some shuteye. We parted ways. I watched his car disappear into the darkness, as the cone of light from his headlights illuminated the rows of corn.

CHAPTER 5

We were ecstatic that we had made it all the way from Lake Point Tower in Chicago to Colorado in a single day—some eight hundred miles. We high-fived each other as our adrenaline gave us a renewed burst of energy. We were now right back on schedule, but we were now in the infamous Middle of Nowhere. It was midnight-dark, except for the sparsely placed streetlights. They illuminated the highway as far as we could see in both directions, and not a single car could be seen nor heard. There was not even a breeze to rustle the cornstalks.

We unrolled our sleeping bags about twenty feet from the highway. Then, a couple minutes later, the first one found us. Then another, and another, and then a never-ending plague of them: mosquitoes. *Gigantic* mosquitoes. They were *hungry* and we were on the menu. In all our careful preparations we never considered insect repellant. After all, above timberline in the Rocky Mountains there simply weren't any insects that bite. Not so in the giant cornfield called Nebraska.

We tried swatting them. We tried hiding in our sleeping bags until the sweltering heat made the tactic unbearable. I had a down bag designed for sub-zero arctic weather, not ninety-degree heat in the middle of summer. We tried smoking a little pot, hoping that the smoke would distract us from our tormentors. That only made it worse—much worse. We learned that marijuana is not a good bug repellent. Finally, in desperation, we rolled up our sleeping bags, walked up to the edge of the road and started walking down the side of the highway. We had to keep up a brisk pace to stay ahead of the cloud of bloodsuckers chasing us. We learned that if we walked down the center of the highway, the cloud behind us would thin out. Maybe the hearty Nebraska mosquitoes had, through natural selection, become street smart.

The bugs still followed us, but if we jogged a little bit we'd leave them behind. It took a while before their brethren down the line realized a blood meal was just twenty feet away. We'd run for a spell, walk for a spell, then lie down for a bit until we couldn't stand it, then repeat the process.

By Wednesday morning we were exhausted. Traffic was still light and we were too tired to offer one-fingered salutes to those who ignored our plight. Finally at about nine o'clock that morning, a van pulled over and offered us a ride. It was a light colored Ford Econoline with a window in each of the two rear swing-out doors. Inside the van there were no seats in the cargo area. Lewis and I gladly took up some floor space behind the front seats. Our packs provided some cushion between our backs and the sides of the van.

The couple who picked us up were going all the way to Denver, and so were we. They were a brother and sister in their twenties. The guy seemed a little bit older than his sister. They were very friendly and pleasant. The woman, being very talkative, spent much of the time turned around in her seat and kneeling so she could face our direction. We had a few hours to kill on the way to Denver and she was curious about our trip. After listening to the tale about our little side-trip to jail in Massachusetts she informed us that the Colorado police, both state and local, were *very* strict about enforcing no-hitchhiking laws.

"Hitching in Colorado is almost guaranteed to land you in jail," she said.

Lewis and I still had a lot of ground to cover and this was not what we wanted to hear. Pondering this, Lewis and I faded off into sleep and didn't wake up until some two hundred miles later when we reached the outskirts of Denver. We had a lot of sleep to catch up on.

As we approached the city, the older brother asked us where we'd like to be dropped off. We told him the YMCA on Colorado Boulevard. The year before, when I was sixteen, I had stayed at the YMCA on my way to the Colorado Outward Bound School. It was the only place I knew of to stay in Denver and it only cost a few dollars per night. Our hosts went out of their way and drove us to the front door and wouldn't accept any money for their efforts. We thanked them profusely. So far in our trip we had found people to be very nice and willing to help us out. We were just two teenagers, maybe a bit naive and way too adventurous, but life was good.

We checked into the YMCA and got our room key. The building was spartan. The walls were cinderblock and the floors in the room and hallways were linoleum tile; our footsteps echoed. To conserve our money, we decided to share a room. The room was about eight feet wide by twelve feet long. There was a window and a single bed up against one wall. Much too small to share. So we did what any two straight guys would do in that situation. Lewis reached in his pocket and pulled out a coin. Whoever won a coin toss would get to sleep in the bed. The loser got the floor.

"Heads or tails?" he said.

I called tails and won. We were both tired and Lewis was not happy about losing the bed for the floor.

After we took showers in the communal bathroom down the hall, we headed out for a late lunch. Over our sandwiches and soft drinks we discussed our next move. Given the warning about hitchhiking in Colorado, and the fact that we had already seen the inside of one jail, we had to find another way to get to Durango. It was about three hundred fifty miles to the southwest, not far from the New Mexico border.

I knew from my travels the previous summer that we could take a bus. Greyhound had daily service to and from Durango. From the restaurant we walked to the bus station to check the schedule and fare. The fare was reasonable—certainly less than paying a fine to get out of jail—so it was an easy decision. I have to admit that I felt a little disappointed. We had made it all the way to Denver by bumming rides, and taking a bus now felt a little like cheating.

The bus would leave at eight in the morning and arrive at Durango about four in the afternoon. We bought our tickets and locked in our travel plans for the following day. It was somewhat of a relief to have solid plans: Instead of just hoping that luck would be with us, we now knew where we'd be tomorrow and how we'd get there. There was no risk of getting arrested or falling prey to some other unanticipated mishap.

During the last few days, we had eaten most of our dehydrated food and GORP (Good Old Raisins and Peanuts, a popular trail mix for hikers). To resupply our rations we stumbled upon Gart Brothers, a sporting goods and camping gear supply store. Back home, the Appalachian Mountain Club store in Boston was about the only place to buy stuff like that. Stores that catered to mountain hiking were commonplace in Colorado, and Gart Brothers was the biggest sporting goods store I had ever seen. They had everything someone would need to climb Mount Everest—tents, hiking boots, skis, and more. Lewis and I bought enough food to stuff our packs with a few days' worth of rations.

While we were shopping for accouterments, we struck up a conversation with a helpful store clerk. We told him where we were from, where we were going, and that we were staying and the YMCA. He mentioned that there was a church not far from the bus station that let people stay for a day or so free. For a night's stay, they only asked for a helping hand from each guest. That sounded better than where we were staying, so we decided we'd give it a try when we arrived back in Denver on the return trip from Durango. We thanked the clerk for the info, stocked up on dehydrated food, got a late lunch, and headed back to the YMCA.

While back at the YMCA, Lewis had an encounter with some of the derelicts who resided there. I suppose we could have been labeled as derelicts, as well, but in our eyes, we were normal. Nature called and Lewis headed to the men's communal restroom. In it was a row of urinals hanging on one wall. The opposite wall had a few sinks and four toilet stalls. Oddly, there were no doors on the stalls. While Lewis was taking care of business in one of the stalls, two black kids walked in and proceeded to sit on the radiator in front of him and watch. Even though there were two of them and only one Lewis, he told them they had better be gone when he finished. They ran out as he was flushing the toilet. As Lewis opened the door to our room he saw them peeking around the corner to see which room he went in. Other than making him angry and a bit disgusted, nothing came of it. We left the YMCA later on that evening for something to eat then came back and went to bed.

Thursday, August 26, and we checked out of the YMCA and arrived at the bus station by seven thirty a.m. There was a coffee shop next door, so we bought a box of donuts and two cups of coffee. Any of the donuts we didn't consume right away would be our snacks for the long bus ride to Durango.

We located our bus in a row of identical buses, all churning out black smoke. We stowed our packs in the cargo area under the bus. It was only accessible by large swing-up doors on the outside of the bus. Upon boarding I mentally noted that the bus was about two-thirds full and most of the passengers were Latino—back in Massachusetts, something unusual. We later realized that Durango, being in the extreme southern part of the state, was home to many Hispanics, and many of the people on the bus were simply going home. We were the foreigners on the bus; we were the only travelers carrying heavy backpacks and we got more than a few curious glances. Other than that, no one paid much attention to us, and no one spoke to us.

It was a boring trip at first, because we were east of the mountains on a fairly flat plain. If you were on the left side of the bus, as we were, you didn't have much of a view. We snoozed through much of it.

Sometime close to noon, the bus driver pulled off the road into an oasis of small shops and a gas station. For some reason obscure to us, it made good economic sense to create a small village at this location. We weren't at the end of the Earth, but you could probably see it from here. So far, I'd noticed that Colorado was pockmarked with abandoned mines, so maybe it was one such mining effort that had first established civilization here.

The bus diver announced that we'd be stopped for about forty-five minutes. It was probably in his contract that he'd be able to take a break from driving. Or maybe it was a requirement. Whatever the reason, it gave Lewis and I enough time to scout out some lunch. Not far from where the bus parked was a greasy spoon restaurant. There was a sign in the door that said NO SHIRT, NO SHOES, NO SERVICE. I thought to myself that it was a good thing the sign didn't mention anything about pants. Lewis's jeans would have gotten us banned.

Along with a few other Greyhound passengers, we ventured into the restaurant and sat down at a small table. A lone waitress meandered between tables and scribbled lunch orders on a pad. I ordered a sandwich and Lewis ordered a hamburger. Included with his meal were a pickle and a bag of potato chips. The waitress said to him, "We're all out of potato chips."

I knew Lewis was frugal, but when he ordered the waitress to "just take fifteen cents off my bill for the chips," I felt a little embarrassed. Especially after seeing the expression on her face. She gave him the what-an-asshole glare before she turned around and stalked off to the kitchen.

The bus ride the previous summer had been full of teenagers like myself, all going to the same place. The Colorado Outward Bound School. We had represented a cross-section of American youth. I was a middle class white guy from New England. There were a few Native American kids, some Denver-area kids, one from Louisiana, and one or more inner city kids from New York and New Jersey. As we'd ridden along in the bus, we'd crested a rise in the terrain. It was our first close-up look at the mountains. One of the city dwellers, a black kid, cried out, "What the hell is that?" It was his first up-close glimpse at a mountain.

Some of us on the bus chuckled, but the huge mountain got even bigger as the bus approached it. In retrospect, it was a mere hill compared to the mountains we all would be climbing in a few days.

Now, with about two thirds of the road to Denver behind Lewis and I, we entered the Rio Grande National Forest. The bus started climbing into the mountains and navigated through some very ominous switchbacks, especially by Treasure Mountain. After about eight hours, which included a number of station stops along the way, the bus arrived in Durango on schedule. Lewis and I departed the bus and collected our backpacks from the chassis compartment. I took a deep breath and stretched out my arms and legs in an attempt to shake out the stiffness. In a few moments, we'd find that just walking a few hundred yards on level ground with heavy backpacks was work. Durango is at an altitude of 6,512 feet above sea level—higher still than Denver.

Durango is literally a railroad town. In 1880 the narrow-gauge Denver and Rio Grande Western Railroad was coming to the area, and the company needed a station to both service the trains and provide a source of water for the steam locomotives. Since a station needs a town, one was built at the direction of retired Union general William Jackson Palmer and his business partner, Dr. William Bell, and they named it Durango. The word "Durango" aptly originates from the Basque word *urango*, which meant "water town." In 1881 the railroad reached Durango and work was begun that Fall on the forty-five-mile stretch to Silverton. On July 11, 1882 the line was finished and opened for business. An engineering marvel, the railway has more than twenty bridges and trestles and its tracks are laid on ledges blasted out of the mountains' rock faces, as it snakes its way through the San Juan National Forest and rises some three thousand feet in elevation. It parallels highway US 550 (merely a dirt track in 1882) and for much of the trip it follows the path of the Animas River. In 1971, the Animas—originally called Rio de las Animas Perdidos, or River of Lost Souls—was one of the few remaining undiverted rivers of more than one hundred miles in length in America, and the only one in Colorado. It was also supposedly tainted with arsenic, a byproduct of the extensive mining operations. We were admonished by the locals not to drink from it.

The main street in Durango looked like the modern version of a cowboy town; something you'd see in movie, except that the street was paved, the buildings were mostly made of brick, and the sidewalks were not wooden. There was a faded sign on the side of a building downtown, announcing the Central Hotel. It was an older building with a light green stucco finish. Any hotel looking this uninviting had to be inexpensive, so Lewis and I ventured from the sidewalk though the front door.

The desk clerk gave us a key to a room on the second floor. At $12 a night, we didn't expect much, and our expectations were granted. On the second story we walked to the end of a long narrow hallway. The floor was wooden and sagged in the middle, maybe from years of wear, or else the lower support structure had weakened from decades of foot traffic. A few residents poked their heads out of their enclaves at the sound of our clanging cooking tins. They were all men, much older than us, who looked as if they were one step above homeless.

It was a small room with a single window, one bed and one cot. I took the cot since Lewis had suffered the floor back at the YMCA in Denver. We were both hungry and ready to find a cooked meal, so we eased the heavy burdens off our backs and left the them behind in the room. As we walked back down the hallway we encountered more stares from gray-haired old men. I had the feeling that these guys could have been long-term residents of the Central Hotel. Lewis and I were being brazenly scrutinized.

We ate dinner at a local restaurant that featured a steak and eggs breakfast special all day long for a very reasonable price. Happy that we were actually at our destination and pretty much on time, we spread out on the restaurant table the topographical maps I had brought with us. For the hundredth time we went over the route we were going to take in the mountains. Sunlight and Windom were the two big peaks—both over fourteen thousand feet—that I wanted to climb. I had ascended both the previous summer. The two mountains stood side-by-side, and there were two small alpine lakes on a plateau fifteen hundred feet or so below the summits. Between the lakes, there was an old shack. The shack was there the summer before, but there were no guarantees that it would still be standing for us. Being above tree line, someone had to have carried all the lumber up to the location between the lakes. There was no way to reach this spot by horse or vehicle. I figured that the shack might have been built and used by a prospector; someplace to get out of the elements while on a mission to find a fortune in the dirt. It would be an ideal camping spot for Lewis and me, if it was still standing.

CHAPTER 6

Friday morning dawned warm and sunny. This was a big day, the day we had traveled two thousand, three hundred, and fifty miles over six days for. Up bright and early, we went back to the restaurant for a second helping of steak and eggs. It would be our last real meal for several days. After cleaning our plates we went back to the hotel, took care of some last-minute business (we wouldn't have indoor plumbing for several days, either), gathered our gear, and checked out. Not far from the hotel was the Durango–Silverton train station.

The coal-fired steam locomotive operates at speeds ranging up to twenty miles per hour. Some of the inside turns are sharp enough that the engine would literally pull the cars off the track at a speed greater than ten miles per hour. As it gains the 3,000 feet in altitude, the engine must pull the train through grades as steep as four percent. While this is child's play for a rack and pinion system like Mount Washington's famous Cog Railway (which can climb an astonishing grade of 37.41 percent), four is about as steep as a conventional train can handle. The train makes two or three stops to take on water to replenish its boiler. The first stop is at the Hermosa tank. At this location a helper engine hooks up to the train. The second stop is at the Tank Creek water tank. The third stop is the Needleton water tank and is optional. Typically, the train only stops to drop off supplies or if there are backpackers who want to get off to go hiking.

The Needleton water tank is on the mountain side of the tracks and deep inside the wilderness of the San Juan Mountain Range. On the other side of the tracks, a few stories below, is the Animas River, a fast-moving mountain stream that swells with the spring runoff. Being August, it was on the low side, but it still looked treacherous and something to be avoided. The summer before, Outward Bound had prearranged that the train would carry our supplies to this stop and unload them.

All the Outward Bound expedition groups had converged the night before and made camp as one unit. We had been several miles away, and a few thousand feet higher than the train tracks. The next morning, we had emptied our backpacks and headed to a much lower altitude without our tents or other equipment behind, with two instructors to look after it all. After having carried heavy backpacks and coiled ropes for two weeks or so, the walk down slope with empty packs had been an easy junket.

An hour or so after leaving camp behind our group had come to the water tank. There, beside the long legs that held up the tank, a few yards from the tracks, were bundles of enough dried food to last for about a week. We each stuffed our empty packs with supplies. The hike back to the camp was a contrast in difficulty. The only consolation was that we'd be able to have a hearty meal when we arrived. At one point along the way, a hunter on horse back passed us on the trail going in the same direction. In cowboy hat and leg chaps, and a rifle strapped to the saddle, he was on his way to the high country in search of elk. With a few strides, that horse caught up to us, passed us, and disappeared into the forest ahead. It made me feel small.

It was from this day's memories at Outward Bound that I had formulated the plans that now lay ahead of Lewis and me. We were the only backpackers onboard the train that day. The engineer was less than thrilled, having to stop at the Needleton tank for two longhaired teenagers.

And Lewis's pants still looked like he had pulled them out of a dumpster. This corner of American hadn't exactly embraced counterculture.

Some of the train cars were open to the weather, but had a roof. Most of the passengers sat in the closed cars, where the smoke from the boiler could be avoided. We sat in the less occupied, last car in the string, an open air observation car. There were fewer people to gawk at us.

A long blow on the whistle and we were moving at last; over US 550, the 15th Street Bridge, and past Huck Finn Pond. We crossed Junction Creek, 32nd Street and 36th Street, then over Trimble Lane to our first stop at the Hermosa tank, some forty minutes after leaving Durango. Here we hooked up to the "helper" engine and filled up with water. After Hermosa the grade steepened as we left civilization behind. We hugged the faces of cliffs, had a view of picturesque Shalona Lake below, and generally enjoyed the incredible scenery. Looking out the back as we crossed a trestle and bridge, we noticed there was nothing between the railroad ties except empty air, and nothing on either side of the tracks—no walkway or railings. I was glad we'd decided not to attempt to walk up the tracks into the mountains, an idea Lewis had come up with to save money. It would have been suicide.

The train made a brief stop at Rockwood, where a few more passengers got on board. Ten minutes later the train entered a narrow rock cut and that opened up into Animas Canyon. We slowed down to traverse the Highline and hugged the face of some very high cliffs. Instinctively, some passengers backed away from the outboard edge. Lewis and I hugged the rail looking down into the canyon below—*way* below. We were getting our money's worth.

A while later, we stopped at Tank Creek to take on more water. A few minutes after leaving, we were on a very narrow rock ledge and entering Cascade Canyon. In the winter, trains had to turn around here due to avalanche danger farther up the line. We again slowed down to less than ten miles per hour as to round yet another sharp curve on the mountain face. A few minutes later we were stopping at Needleton water tank.

Back at the ticket office we had stated our intentions to get off the train there. The tickets were priced accordingly. As we approached the water tank, the already slow train crept to a halt. Since all of the other passengers were tourists, Lewis and I became the focus of their attention as we climbed off the train under the weight of our backpacks, sleeping bags, tent, and cooking gear. A number of people pointed their cameras in our direction and took our picture. We had become part of the local color, immortalized anonymously.

We stood beside the tracks next to the water tank and watched as the train struggled to start moving again. The sound of escaping steam was deafening as the engineer released the brakes and the engine began to chug. The cadence of the chugging increased as the train began to pick up momentum. The train had stopped on a grade steep enough that a layer of sand had to be put on the tracks for traction—otherwise, the steel wheels would just spin and the train would go nowhere. Sand is actually much harder than steel; it consists mostly of quartz, which is a 7 on the Mohs hardness scale compared to steel's 6. Under the immense pressure of the K-36 locomotive's 286,600 pounds, the tiny grains bit into both rail and wheel, thus increasing friction. To better his chances, the engineer backed the train up a foot while the rear brakeman still had his brakes on, compressing all the couplings. This reduced the load the engine had to pull for that all-important first second when the wheels began to turn. Once underway, the train began the final three and a half hours to Silverton.

We had been blissfully unaware of all the complexities of operating a steam locomotive that sunny morning on August 27, when we boarded the train. All we cared about was the fact that we were here, and soon would be There—on foot and climbing to the top of the world, or at least what seemed like the top of the world to us.

Again oblivious to the tourists watching us, with the train to our backs, we got our bearings and spotted the same rope bridge over the Animas River that I had crossed the year before. Albeit a year older, it looked the same and just as ominous. It was a narrow but sturdy rope bridge. It has wooden slats for a platform, and was suspended twenty feet above the swift river and stretched some one hundred feet in length. It swayed in response to our combined weight and we realized why it was narrow. To prevent falling you needed to be able to hang on to *both* rope railings as you crossed. It was strictly one-way.

While on the side of the river opposite the tracks, we took a moment to sniff the river mist for any sign of arsenic. We didn't detect any odor—as if either of us knew what arsenic smelled like, or if it even had an odor. We congratulated ourselves, proud that we had wisely filled our canteens before leaving Durango. With the river behind us we headed north towards Ruby Creek and the trail that winds along it, the same trail I had hiked the previous year. It is late morning and we wanted to cover as much ground as we could before setting up camp for the night.

The virgin forest was dense. There was not much undergrowth, but towering trees reached amazing heights in their life-and-death competition to capture their share of energy from sunshine. We passed through a few stands of aspen trees and then some tall Ponderosa pines higher up the trail. The only open ground was along rivers and creeks until we reached the timberline, which would not be till tomorrow. We were already at about 8,600 feet, some two thousand feet higher than Durango, and could really feel the difference. There simply was not as much oxygen, and we are mindful not to exert ourselves until we got acclimated.

The Ruby Creek trail was a relatively gentle and a manageable incline. The uphill side was to our left and a stream ran down the slope on our right. These trails were maintained by the Forest Service. Since I had been there last, they had cleared a fifty-yard section of the trail of some debris deposited by either a winter avalanche or a massive rockslide. Looking up to our left, there was a gash in the forest that looked like a tornado trail. Enormous pine trees were flung around like matchsticks among automobile-sized boulders.

As we climbed, we found ourselves taking more frequent breaks. We'd spend a few minutes resting our aching muscles and catching our breath. We pressed on for a couple of hours then decided to call it a day in a small meadow beside the creek. The terrain was sloping, but we found an eight-by-ten-foot area where the ground was almost level and free of stones. There was a patch of grass, a much nicer mattress than granite. Boulders sheltered our campsite. The sun was low in the sky and the tall Ponderosas cast long shadows. The forest had become so dark that we couldn't see past the closest tree trunks. It gave me the creeps. I knew that there were animals in there larger and stronger than we were, but hopefully not very hungry. From previous experience, I expected to hear the screeching and cackling of hungry coyotes during the night. Lewis and I reminded each other that in this forest we were no longer at the top of the food chain.

We pitched my two-man, international orange tent on the grass just inside the forest, maybe fifty feet from the creek. I told Lewis, "We may not be the only creatures drinking from the creek and we don't want to crowd anyone." Especially at night, which falls incredibly quickly. Lewis had expected to see spectacular sunsets and was disappointed, but I already knew that it just gets dark. There's no light pollution and little moisture in the atmosphere this high up, so far from civilization. And we were on the wrong side of the mountain.

Making a temporary camp has a certain routine. While I rolled out our sleeping bags in the tent I instructed Lewis to collect a few dozen softball-sized stones and place them in a circle about three feet in diameter. We then foraged the surrounding area for dead, dried tree branches to fuel a fire. It didn't take long to have a crackling campfire. We took two Y-shaped branches, about a foot tall, and propped them with the fork end up at opposite sides of the fire pit. We laid a freshly cut length of branch in the two Y's and hung a can full of water over the fire. The idea was to have boiling water before the fresh branch caught fire. One of us had to tend the fire and be ready to retrieve the can in case the branch didn't last.

With the boiling water, we hydrated some food and ate our first dinner in the wilderness. It reminded me of my Outward Bound days when we had pitched camp in a different alpine location every night for a month. Breakfast and dinner were made this way every day. At breakfast, by the time one of us had made a fire and cooked a meal for several people, others would have rolled up all the sleeping bags and someone would have collapsed and packed every tent. No time was wasted. We always had a long hard day of mountaineering to deal with. Before we left a campsite, we'd douse the fire, scatter the stones from the fire pit and make the area look as it did when we found it.

After dinner, Lewis and I filled our canteens from nearby creek, munched some trail mix for dessert, and climbed into our sleeping bags.

CHAPTER 7

Morning breaks about as abruptly as night falls. Neither of us slept well due to the altitude and dryness of the air. Since we were on sun-time now, we got up at first light, took care of business, and ate a light breakfast. As we refilled our canteens in the creek we saw that visitors had been there during the night: bears. Their paw prints were deep in the soft bank and *big*. Almost as big as our boot prints. The scary thing is how far the claws extended from the rest of the print. Save for two small hunting knives we were completely unarmed. Mindful of the fact that bears rarely went above timberline, we broke camp and got moving.

Hiking got more difficult the higher we climbed. We were at an altitude somewhere close to eleven thousand feet, and we two sea-level boys were feeling it. We mostly hiked in silence, puffing for breath. Breaks were frequent, as were headaches and bloody noses due to the dryness.

I've heard it said that at twelve thousand feet, simply walking on level ground is like carrying a fifty-pound pack.

Considering that we actually were carrying fifty-pound packs and not on level ground, the going was tough. I'd look down, raise a leg, put one foot in front of the other, and repeat the process. Fortunately our legs were in good shape. I did a lot of skiing in the winter and Lewis spent a whole summer carrying bricks and mortar up a ladder while working for his uncle (Lewis's uncle primarily built chimneys). As we reached the headwaters of the creek we faced a couple of fairly steep slopes ahead. On the steep parts, the trail zigzagged back and forth to lessen the grade, but it doubled the distance traveled. Factoring in breaks and the traverse, we figured we were traveling, at best, one mile an hour.

The surroundings were familiar to me. As we approached the tree line at around twelve thousand feet, the grade became much steeper. I remembered that the next hour or more of climbing would test us both. Me, for the second time. At least I knew what to expect. From here we could see the surrounding mountain peaks. There were acre-sized patches of snow that were shaded from the sun most of the day. In our path, between us and our destination, was a steep alpine meadow—so steep in places that you could stand up straight, stretch your arm out in front of you and touch the ground.

Our only fuel for cooking was wood. We had not packed any type of camping stove. This wasn't an oversight. Along the highways we could eat at local restaurants and buy snacks at gas stations. I knew we could do just fine without a camping stove because I had lived in the mountains for a month without one last summer. We could find wood when and where we needed it. However, our next few nights would be spent above the timberline.

I hadn't mentioned this to Lewis until now. We stopped to rest at the tree line, where the grade of slope took a sharp tilt upward. It was a good place to take our packs off and have a sip of water and catch our breath.

"Lewis, we need to gather wood here so we have firewood to burn at the next campground," I explained. I watched his facial expression morph from "What are you talking about?" to "Oh yeah, that makes sense" to "You gotta be kidding me. We have to carry firewood up THAT slope?" For the next twenty minutes we foraged in the immediate area until we had more wood than we could carry. We tied the small branches into bundles and strapped them to the tops of our backpacks. Now we had another ten pounds or so to deal with.

Lewis looked at me and said, "Whose idea was this camping trip, anyway?"

For what seemed like eternity, we took one step at a time, lugging those heavy backpacks on our backs up hill. We assisted our climbing with walking sticks. They helped us balance and we leaned on them during our frequent stops. Besides, we could use them as fuel later on.

When we reached the top of the slope, we were greeted by a scene that made the day's struggle worth every heart-beating, head-aching second. In front of us was a panorama of stone and sky. In the forefront was an alpine lake reflecting the palette of nature's beauty. The sun was still high in the sky. The air was cool, and the sunshine was warm. Not a breeze could be felt and the lake was a perfect mirror. Beyond it was a solid wall of rock hundreds of feet tall and perfectly vertical. Its jagged edge scratched the sky, contrasting with wispy clouds. On the other side of the lake, still standing, was the tiny shack I had visited the previous summer. I pondered how it could have survived. It must have spent an uncounted number of winters under tens of feet of snow. Somehow it persisted. This would be our home, our shelter, and our base camp for the next three days.

From our vantage point, we couldn't see the other alpine lake, which lay just beyond the stone ledge the shack was perched on. But I knew it was there, nestled in at the bottom of the stone cathedral behind it. There were still patches of snow scattered around like randomly placed throw rugs. The lakes were the puddles left over from the snowmelt. The water was a complex mixture turquoise blue, green, and reflected images from the surroundings. This was ground zero. Our ultimate destination. We had made it here all the way from the Massachusetts shore. A few unexpected detours had almost scuttled our plans, but we were here, and we were excited.

The adrenaline was just what we needed to forget about the thin air for a few minutes and lift us over the last stretch of declining slope to the plateau and then to the edge of the closest lake.

As we walked along the shore toward the cabin, Lewis exclaimed, "Too bad you left your fishing pole in that car."

"There's no fish up here, anyway, but a trout for dinner would be nice."

The lakes, I later learned, are appropriately named Twin Lakes. We were in the Needle Mountains, a subrange of the San Juan Mountains. And it's all located in the Weminuche Wilderness, which is part of the San Juan National Forest in La Plata County. There are three fourteen-thousand-foot mountains in the Needle Mountains; Sunlight Peak, Mount Eolus, and Windom Peak. Windom and Sunlight are just east of Twin Lakes, in upper Chicago Basin, and Eolus lies on the west.

As we approached the cabin, the memories of last summer came to focus in my mind's eye. Twelve months earlier I had stood in the same place, taken in the same beauty and felt blessed to be alive. We were in an area incredibly remote by even Colorado standards.

Cabin was really too good a word. Shack is better. It was a dilapidated structure, about six by ten feet, with a threshold at one end but no door. The rusted corrugated metal roof would keep out most of the rain. The walls had holes and spaces between the wooden slats where the wind and weather blew through. There was debris on the dirt floor, straw and sticks, and we had to do some house cleaning to clear sites big enough to unroll our sleeping bags. Where the roof came to a peak, the ceiling was tall enough for an average person to stand up straight. The doorway, however, required us to duck. Even so, it was better than being outside and it provided more room than my two-man tent. I reminded myself that someone had to have carried all the building material up here.

We could see the three fourteeners from the shack: towering stone behemoths. I had ascended to the summits of Sunlight and Windom last summer. Stashed among the rocks at the peaks was a section of pipe about a foot long, capped with screw caps at both ends, that held a scroll of paper and a pencil. It was a register where climbers recorded their ascents by signing and dating their accomplishment. We'd try to find these in the next couple of days.

Lewis ran over to the lake in front of our new home intent on going for a swim, until he realized glacial lakes were way too cold to swim in. Instead we unpacked some of our gear and set up shop as best we could. We relaxed for a bit and then did some exploring.

The day was still graced with sunshine. A few wispy clouds moved slowly and closely past the peaks of the Needle Mountains. Needle was a good description: They were spires hundreds of feet high with pointed tips that resembled a stand of arborvitaes.

There was a large snowfield ascending a gorge between Sunlight and Windom Peaks, which we explored in the early afternoon sunshine. Soon, though, the weather changed to predictable rain and hail showers. The wind whipped up, pelting Lewis and I with soft rain and stinging hail. The shack became our refuge. We sat listening to the ice pellets snap against the steel roof. Lewis unfolded a topographical map. As we pinpointed our location, we were still in awe of our journey. We planned our next move, the ascent of Sunlight Peak.

After the weather subsided we made a small campfire. Our fuel supply had to be rationed. We needed heat to boil water to prepare our dehydrated meals, and neither of us wanted to climb back down to the tree line for more kindling. A fire for any other purpose was just a luxury.

The water from Twin Lakes was crystal clear and appeared to be safe to drink. Lewis expressed his concern that it might contain minerals that could make us sick, but I assuaged his fear by reminding him that I had cooked with water from the same source the previous summer. Compared to sea level, water boiled at a lower temperature up here. This was because the air pressure was lower at high elevations; boiling occurs when the water is hot enough to create a vapor pressure equal to the pressure of the surrounding atmosphere. At high altitudes, air pressure is lower than at sea level, so the water doesn't have to get as hot to reach boiling.

Likewise, our dinners were less than stellar. In order for dehydrated food to taste its best, it had to be boiled hard for at least three minutes, then left to set for a while as the cooking process finished. Along the way, our food had been pretty tasty, but at this altitude water boiled at about 185 degrees. That temperature difference made our dinners taste like lukewarm mush.

The next morning we woke at first light. We were still on a daylight schedule—up at dawn, in bed at dusk. The air was cool and crisp, not a cloud in the sky; a perfect day for ascending Sunlight Peak.

The trail was clearly marked with cairns built by previous climbers to mark the way. The path was strewn with loose rocks and boulders, and an occasional patch of snow. Steeper sections were covered with small rocks called scree. Scree was the sound they made when your foot put pressure on them and ground them against each other. We were happy to have left our heavy gear at the base camp, but the altitude and low oxygen level made the climbing almost as tiresome as at lower altitudes with a heavy pack. We were carrying only canteens and some candy bars. We knew that the temperature higher up might be much cooler, so we put on extra layers of clothing.

The view from the top was spectacular. You could see, literally, for a hundred miles. The crenelated landscape was majestic with peaks and valleys, ridges and ravines, creeks and rivers. At this height and distance it was hard to pick out any sign of civilization. Using our map and nearby peaks as reference points, we could surmise where the various towns were, but at best they appeared as little smudges, and usually were obscured by the tremendous peaks. Those little smudges may have been Dayfield, Pogosa Springs, Telluride, or even Durango. Since man-made roads usually take the path of least resistance, they lay in the valleys between the mountains and were hence invisible to us. We could have been on the moon, or thrown into a distant past beyond remembrance.

Less than two miles to the east was the Continental Divide. Theoretically, water that falls on the western side of the divide eventually ends up in the Pacific Ocean, and water that falls on the eastern side eventually ends up in the Atlantic. Looking down from fourteen thousand feet, the valley floors appeared to be carpeted with green pool table felt. Patches of snow dotted the landscape in areas where shadows from the mountain peaks dominated most of each day. We could see a beautiful blue lake down there, its azure color contrasting the green alpine meadow. If I had not left my fishing pole in that guy's car, I might have wanted to try to catch some golden rainbow trout that supposedly you can only find in lakes above six thousand feet.

At the peak we thought we'd celebrate our accomplishment and smoke a little pot. It turned out to be a bad idea. At that altitude, the effect was greatly magnified. And given the remoteness of our location, we could hardly dial 9-1-1 even if an emergency number had been available in 1971. We were terrified we'd hurt ourselves if we attempted to descend, so we simply sat, afraid to move, and waited for the effect to wear off.

Because of the cyclical and very predictable weather pattern, we needed to get back to base camp before the clouds moved in and released their torrent of hail on our heads.

Up to this point, the entire journey had been uphill. Paradoxically, climbing down is much harder and can be more dangerous than hiking up, especially if you are carrying a heavy pack. It's more difficult to lean backward than forward, so it's easier to lose your footing and equally easy to get going too fast—and then, the only way to brake is to fall down. You use a totally different set of leg muscles, most of which are not nearly as strong as the ones you use climbing. Add to this the psychological fact that you're looking straight down a few thousand feet. When ascending, you are staring at the rocks in front of your face, or straight across a few miles to another fourteen-thousand-foot peak.

We agreed to take our time, no matter how long it took. So we carefully began the descent, traversing where we could, and constantly looked for secure footing. We had our share of missteps, but fortunately we fell backward and not forward. Sometimes we actually slid on the seat of our pants to get to a more stable spot. We rested frequently and tried to ignore the headache that comes from the exertion, the altitude, and the extreme tension we felt in every muscle. From a distance we must have looked like Lewis's grandmother crossing an icy street. Finally, we made it to our shack at base camp, just in time to take cover from the late-day hailstorm.

For the remainder of daylight we sat tight in our tiny enclave and tried to stay dry and warm. As dusk approached we made a small fire, always careful to conserve our fuel, and cooked up another delightful meal of rehydrated mush.

The next day we rose again with the sun. Before us was the day's planned journey: conquering our second fourteen-thousand-foot peak, Sunlight Peak. The morning sky was clear blue and the air cool and refreshing. There was not even a hint of a breeze; the sun had not yet worked its magic, heating the different layers and pockets of air, which would start shifting the air masses.

After a quick breakfast of dry snacks chased with cold lake water, we laid out our map to find the best route up Sunlight. Even though I had climbed it before, I wasn't sure the route had been the best.

In hindsight, the two of us were incredibly naive about safety. As two young males, especially two guys who had just hitchhiked across the country, we felt indestructible. What could happen that we couldn't deal with? But with no cell phones or other means of communication, an injury might strand one of us in the mountains for days. If we were both injured severely enough that neither of us could go for help, we'd face death. We hadn't left an itinerary with anyone. No one knew where we were, other than someplace in the San Juan National Forest.

After breakfast, we started out by retracing our hike from the previous day. The additional day of acclimating to the high altitude had no effect on me. Breathing was still difficult and my legs ached even worse than they did yesterday. Even so, the adrenaline in my system took over, the awesome scenery occupied my mind, and I felt as though I had just landed on the moon.

We crossed several acre-sized patches of snow, crunching along in yesterday's footprints. The snow was granular, like the corn snow I had skied on so many times back East during spring skiing. Once we neared the ravine's upper end, we veered left toward Sunlight Peak. Windom and Sunlight stood side by side like sentries protecting the valley floor, hundreds if not thousands of feet below. At 14,000 feet, they are among the tallest peaks in the lower forty-eight states.

We ascended along the cairns that marked the trail. The climb was noticeably steeper than the way to the top of Windom Peak—or maybe it just seemed so because our muscles were sore. But the work earned us another breathtaking view from the summit. Windom stood nearby. The breeze was still. The morning was so quiet that if there was someone on top of Windom, we might have been able to yell across the emptiness and have a conversation.

Among the loosely strewn boulders at the top I spotted a marmot. He would cautiously eye us and then disappear between the rocks. A few seconds later he would poke his head up and take another look at us.

I commented to Lewis, "I wonder what a marmot finds to eat way up here?" Lewis had spotted a large bird soaring up the valley on the air currents, banking from side to side to avoid colliding with the mountains. "I don't know what a marmot eats, but I bet that bird eats fresh marmot."

The avian navigator was too far away for me to identify, but could have been an eagle.

We had learned our lesson the day before, so we didn't celebrate our feat with a joint this time. We just sat on the peak for a half hour or so. Our every movement was careful: A wrong step could result in a fatal drop, and my slight fear of heights was a healthy, self-preserving phobia right now. Even so, the view was so captivating that we lingered as long as we felt we could. If the weather was going to repeat itself again today, we knew we should give ourselves plenty of time to descend so as not to be caught in the hail and rain.

The descent was like yesterday's, except that the tops of my thighs hurt worse than before. On one or more of the snow patches, Lewis and I each took a turn at slipping and landing on our respective ass; only the quick instinct to dig in our heels saved us from accelerating toward the rocks at the lower end of the snowfield.

We made it back to the shack between the lakes at early afternoon, just like the day before. We were tired but exhilarated. After all, we had accomplished what we had set out to do. We had hitchhiked more than two thousand miles, and climbed two of the tallest peaks in the southern Rockies. We were a little melancholic because, for now, it seemed like the best was behind us. We had only to look forward to the long journey home—and there was no pot of gold at the end of that rainbow.

The afternoon storm came and went. The rain dripped on us sporadically between the metal roof slats and the temperature dropped. When the storm moved out of the valley, Lewis and I made a small fire and cooked dinner. We still had a decent supply of firewood, so we didn't have to be as stingy with it. This would be our last night in the mountains. The sun went down soon after the fire died out. The stars dotted the black sky. Lewis and I lay in our sleeping bags under the tin roof, reflecting on the last two days. I slipped into sleep not long after Lewis started snoring. The next day, we would break camp and head down hill, then north to Denver and east toward home.

CHAPTER 8

Tuesday, August 31, 1971, dawned as sunny as all the others. We had a busy day ahead of us, so we had something to eat and broke camp early. The train would be coming through at about 2:30 p.m. and we wanted to make sure we were there with time to spare. It wouldn't wait for us if we were late—the railroad engineer didn't know we'd be meeting him that day, anyway. We had only the station employee's assurance that the train would stop at the water tank if we made ourselves obvious. The plan was to arrive early, wave our arms, and jump up and down.

It was probably only seven miles as the crow flies from our camp to the Needleton Tank stop, but we weren't crows and we couldn't fly. The twisting and turning trail over countless traverses lengthened the path ahead of us into at least ten miles, maybe more. This time, however, we'd have gravity working with us, not against us. We'd be able to cover twice the distance in the same amount of time it took to ascend.

With the Twin Lakes to our backs, we trudged to the edge of the plateau, overlooking the steep alpine meadow we had climbed a few days before with our packs laden with food and firewood. Most of our food had been consumed and the little fuel we hadn't used, we left behind for some someone else. We cleared away all traces of our visit and took extra effort to leave it as we had found it.

The human body may get somewhat acclimated to this altitude, but the fact remains that there are forty percent fewer molecules of oxygen per breath than at sea level. You breathe faster, and thus get dehydrated quickly. The lack of oxygen also gave us headaches and bloody noses. Sleeping was difficult. Sometimes I'd wake up in the middle of the night gasping for air. My overall energy level seemed to decrease every day. We had originally planned to spend a few more days at Twin Lakes, but we were tired and ready to head home.

We took a last look back toward the lakes and then started our descent through the steep meadow, along the traversing pathway. As we headed down, we had another stunning view of the Rockies. A mile or more away were the peaks at the other side of the valley. I had crossed over them the previous summer. Below us, several hundred feet down, was the top canopy of the coniferous forest—the tall spires of the Ponderosa pines. We could make out the ribbon of our trail slithering like a snake into the cover of the forest beyond the grassy meadow.

In less than an hour we were under those trees, and once again, were dwarfed and awed by their stature. A while later we passed the grassy area where we had camped Friday night. It was only four days ago, but it now seemed like weeks.

In comparison to climbing, the descent was a pleasurable stroll. In the reverse direction we'd been sweating and huffing and puffing so much that conversation just wasn't worth the extra effort. Now, we could talk and focus our thoughts on topics other than how much we ached. The beauty of the forest became much more important, as we could look out ahead of us. After a while, we passed the area, now on our right, that had been devastated by a rockslide or avalanche within the past year. This also gave us a landmark along our journey to the railway.

Lewis looked at me and burst a quick staccato, "Shh!"

We both stopped and listened.

After a moment he said, "I thought I heard some voices."

I was relieved. My mind had envisioned a bear or wildcat, and my heart had already started pounding.

"There it is again," he said.

Sure enough, this time I heard voices as well. Female voices.

We were not expecting any human contact until we reached the train. The voices got closer and then two young women appeared, walking through the trees. They were in their mid to late twenties. Both had dark hair and were wearing shorts. They only had light knapsacks, a stark contrast to the large heavy packs Lewis and I wore. One was tall, the other compact, but both obviously athletic and in good shape. Most astonishing of all was the fact that the shorter one was carrying a small dog!

They seemed as surprised as us by a human encounter on this trail. At first, we just stood and looked at them and they at us.

Finally I broke the stalemate and said, "So I guess it wasn't a bear you heard, Lewis."

The gals smiled and probably understood what I was talking about.

Our collective curiosity took over and we started asking one another what we were doing here, where we had come from, and so forth. We learned that the women worked for the railway and had asked a friend to drive them up as far up a dirt road as he could go with his jeep and let them off. They then hiked for a while, spent the night in a blanket-style bedroll, got up the next morning, and were making their way to the train. They had been south of us in the lower elevations, but still at a respectable eleven to twelve thousand feet up. They had just decided they wanted to get outdoors for a couple of days.

We were impressed that two young women would head out cross-country with virtually no supplies and no map that we could see, and spend the night under the stars with just a puppy for protection—a puppy that had to be carried, no less. And they were able to locate the train by dead reckoning. Impressive! We walked together to the Needleton water tank, crossed the arsenic-laced Animas River, shared our respective stories, and sat at the side of the tracks waiting for the train to show up. It was nice to have some new friends to talk with. Lewis and I had been each other's sole company for long enough. Two attractive females were a boon—even though they were older than us, they hung on every word from our satchel of travel stories.

In due course we heard the chuffing sound of the steam locomotive in the distance. It soon pulled into view from what looked like a black hole in the forest. The train was laden with tourists and once again we passed into legend as everyone on the train snapped pictures of the two attractive young women with the cute little puppy and the two very dirty mountain men with the huge backpacks. Lewis was still wearing those stupid jeans, and very much looked the part of someone who had been raised by wolves in the wilderness. And now he smelled like it, too.

The train came to a stop and the engineer and fireman scurried around, checking this and oiling that. We boarded the car that had stopped closest to us and once again made our way to the back. A few tourists came up and asked what we had been doing, and we described our trip without embellishments. Our trek had been adventurous enough that there was no need to exaggerate. After we answered their questions, the tourists were careful to stay upwind of us. The train lurched and we began the two-hour ride back to Durango.

This time, instead of the quivering excitement of anticipation, I felt a bit wistful, knowing the best part was over. We were on the return trip, the downslope of a natural high. The specter of the 2,350-mile trip we had ahead of us was already starting to loom. We had to retrace every mile of highway. It began to sink in as the train retraced its own journey. We steamed over all the same, narrow bridges and trestles and hugged the same rock faces we had hugged just a few days ago.

Tourists jostled from the rail on one side of the car to the opposite rail to catch the best view. Lewis and I simply looked out. We had seen much grander vistas above the timberline. When we approached the station, the engineer sounded the train whistle one last long blow. It was a sound we would never hear again.

We climbed down from the train car. Our new friends were right behind us. Lewis and I took a moment to say our goodbyes. Shouldering our backpacks, we trudged down Durango's main street to the Central Hotel. Back here at 6,500 feet above sea level, we now felt energetic, almost high, from the extra oxygen. Our bodies had been trying so hard to adjust to life at twice this altitude that now we had a spring in our step, even with heavy backpacks.

When we arrived at the Central Hotel we checked in and then took the first shower we'd had in five days.

Afterward, we went out for an early dinner. It tasted like gourmet food, at least compared with the lukewarm mush we'd been eating up in the mountains. With our bellies full and our appetites sated, the long day was beginning to catch up to us, so we headed back to our room.

While we were getting our gear packed for the early bus ride to Denver the next day, the taller woman stopped by our room. She talked to us for a bit, said how glad she was to meet people who loved the mountains as much as she did, and told us to look her up if we were ever back in Durango. She gave us her name and address: Janet James, 225 First Street, Durango, and then left. Something of her presence lingered, and I found myself reflecting on the fact that something about Janet was very attractive.

Lewis and I woke up early the next morning, refreshed, relaxed, and ready to trek to the bus station. It was time to head home.

After stuffing the last few items into our packs, we checked out of the hotel and then went for breakfast at a small restaurant on the main drag. We arrived at the bus station with time to spare, bought our tickets, and waited for departure time. For some reason, there didn't seem to be as many passengers heading for Denver as there were on the bus ride in.

When the time came to board our bus, we remembered to sit on the left side so we'd have the best scenery on the trip. The driver took us through the same mountains and switchbacks and drove out to the eastern plain by late morning. Lewis and I relaxed our sore muscles during the long trip north to Denver, where we arrived about four that afternoon. While on the bus, a passenger, a guy about our age, reminded us about the church in Denver where street people and travelers of our ilk could spend the night for free. Like a youth hostel, all we had to do were some chores. Lewis and I decided to check it out. It would save us a few bucks, and we were running short on cash.

The bus ride back to Denver from the Outward Bound base camp the previous year had been much more entertaining. It was a party on wheels. Before we boarded the bus, the staff, true to their word, returned each bag of recreational drugs that they had collected on the first day of camp; and the party started before the bus turned the corner from the dirt camp road onto the highway. After a few miles, the smoke in the bus was so thick that I wondered if the whole thing would lift off the ground. The driver must have known what to expect, because he never objected to what was going on in his rear view mirror. We had just survived the most physically demanding and psychologically stressful month of our teenage lives. We didn't know it then, but our participation would have an enduring influence on our futures—in the decisions we made and the confidence we would apply to our journeys in life. The boundaries we would apply to our dreams had been widened by discovering our limits.

When Lewis and I arrived in Denver, we stepped off the bus, got our bearings, and found a city map on the wall in the bus station. Behind a glass panel was a map of Denver. On the map we located the free church where we were planning to stay. The street address wasn't too far to walk from the red "You Are Here" sticker. No bus or taxi would deplete our dwindling supply of cash. We set our bearing for the church, hefted our packs over our shoulders and headed out onto the cement sidewalk.

The church was an older building in the middle of the city. A dozen or more people were milling around outside. None of them looked very friendly—street bums, mostly. We fit right in.

Lewis approached one man who at least looked sober, and confirmed that this was the church that opened its doors for people to spend the night. He also asked him where we could find the pastor. The guy pointed in the general direction of where he thought the pastor might be.

So on we went, through the church and out into an open courtyard where we found him. He gave us the once-over and then resumed what he was doing, whatever that was. He was a thin man, medium height, with black hair and very intense eyes. A razor blade hadn't touched his face for at least a couple of days. He was holding a cup of black coffee. We later learned that he was a recovering alcoholic and drank prodigious amounts of caffeine. I think he felt a camaraderie with the street drunks. He had probably been one himself and was happy to give a helping hand to those who were walking in his old shoes.

We introduced ourselves and indicated we'd like to stay the night and that we were willing to help out where we could. He gave us a nod and pointed his finger at a guy who would give us direction. Our assignment, our fee for a night in the church, was to help clean up after dinner, which would be in a few minutes. That must have been why all the bums were standing outside of the church. Free food. We hadn't known about the free meal, so to us it was a bonus.

We ate buffet style in the auditorium with a number of other people. All of us were sitting on plastic chairs and eating at folding rectangular tables that seated eight. Lewis and I had stashed our backpacks against the wall of the auditorium and we took pains to keep watch over them. We were back in the real world now, and had to exercise our street smarts.

Sitting with us at our table was a guy and his girlfriend, both our age. We started talking. Over dinner we told them our story of where we had come from, what we had done, and how we needed to get back to Boston. Our new acquaintances corroborated what we had been told about hitchhiking being illegal in Colorado. We told them the episode of how we had already seen the inside of one jail and didn't want to see the inside of another. The couple told us they were stopping for the night here in Denver, at the church, and were driving up to Cheyenne, Wyoming the next day. They asked if we wanted to come along with them and of course we said yes—if for no reason but to get out of Colorado. It was a little out of our way, but it would at least get us out of the state. They said they'd be happy to drive us if we could help them out with a few dollars for gas. We agreed to split a tank of gas with them and thanked them for their offer.

After dinner we helped clear tables, and with a few other vagabonds we stacked the chairs, folded the tables, and moved them all into a storage area.

It was still early in the evening, so we walked around a bit and kept our packs with us. We learned that the sleeping area was in the church. I mean, really in the church: on and between pews, in the aisle, and anywhere one could find space. We turned in early. As we entered the sleeping area, the pastor was assigning sleeping spots. Some places, such as on the pews, were the more coveted locations and had probably resulted in turf skirmishes in the past. The pastor was there to keep the peace.

I guess I was one of the lucky ones, because he assigned me a pew where I could stretch out and not be on the hard floor. Lewis became the occupier of a piece of the floor next to the wall and near a doorway. Our friends, the girlfriend boyfriend duo, slept on only a couple of blankets. Across the room was an American Indian with incredibly long black hair and a big dog, some kind of husky. To our surprise, the Indian stripped completely naked before he slipped into his sleeping bag. The dog didn't bother anyone but you could tell Fido did not like the three black guys who were sleeping a few feet away. It appeared that they didn't like the Indian much, either.

After everybody was settled, someone flipped the light switch off and the church became almost black. A sound began to emanate from one of God's children. It sounded like it came from the guy on the floor in front of the next pew. On his every exhale, he hummed a monotone note. The next exhale repeated the same sound. After a few of these, the others began to stir. I heard some rumbling voices and an angry, "What the fuck?" The next monotone exhale was answered with a loud, "Shut up!" from somewhere in the gallery.

The neighbor who occupied the space behind me stood up, leaned over the back of my pew and growled in my face, "Shut up or I'll kick your ass." I quickly saved my ass by responding, "It's not me, brother." After the next hum from whomever, I heard the thud of a foot or fist against flesh. The annoying hum went silent for the rest of the night.

I soon fell asleep, but awoke a few hours later to the noise of scuffle between the Indian and the black guys. Someone turned the lights on. The dog was growling and then some other guys escorted the black guys from the auditorium. Things quieted down again and we fell back asleep.

Morning came and we looked for the guy and his girlfriend. Fortunately they hadn't hit the road without us.

The church didn't provide breakfast so the four of us got food en route. As promised, we helped them fill their tank with gas and we made our way to Interstate 25. We drove north a hundred miles to Cheyenne, Wyoming. An hour and a half later we had reached Interstate 80. We said our goodbyes, and they dropped us off a hundred feet after the entrance ramp to I-80. We shouldered our packs and walked to the eastbound side.

We were in Wyoming, where hitchhiking on the highway was okay. Or so we thought. Because of the high-speed traffic merging onto I-80 from northbound I-25, we had to walk the better part of a mile east on the highway so that any potential rides would have no difficulty pulling over to pick us up.

We soon got our first ride, a short hop that at least got us away from the intersection with I-25. We claimed a piece of pavement and stuck our thumbs out again. Surrounding us on all sides was prairie, brown prairie. The grass had been burned by the hot summer sun. The landscape was mildly rolling and obscured the view in some directions. We could, however, clearly see the ribbon of highway for at least a mile behind us. One hundred feet or so to the east was a dirt road leaving the highway from the eastbound side. Where the road met the highway, there was a row of mailboxes. There must have been some houses down that dirt road, but the rolling landscape blocked them from our view. To our east, in the direction of our travel, was a rise in the prairie about a mile out that obscured our vision. There were no buildings in view except a few tall grain silos on the horizon.

The morning gave way to the hot afternoon sun. An occasional game of gin rummy helped us kill time. Traffic was very light and not particularly friendly. Hours passed and we alternated our positions, one of us standing in the breakdown lane with thumb out, and the other sitting down in the grass a few yards back.

Once you get a few miles east of I-25 on I-80, you're into farm and ranch country, where the traffic is sparse and fast. We soon got the impression that the locals didn't much care for longhaired teens like us. One car went by and someone threw a beer bottle at us. Fortunately, it missed. At eighty miles an hour, a direct hit could have been fatal. Another pickup truck went by and threw a lit firecracker at us. We both jumped when it exploded near our feet. Other vehicles passed, and their occupants hollered at us. We couldn't make out the words but we were certain they weren't friendly.

After a few more hours of this, we were getting pretty discouraged. Just then, a slim and attractive lady walked toward us along the dirt driveway to retrieve her mail from one of the mailboxes. Her body language communicated apprehension when she spotted us—Lewis with his garbage pants, our long hair, and our clothes and packs soiled with days of road dirt. Lewis and I were close enough to the mailboxes to offer a greeting to the woman.

"Where are you boys going?" she asked.

In unison we answered, "Chicago."

"I don't know why anyone would ever want to go to that place," she replied. Then she turned around and walked back down the dirt road until she disappeared behind a swell in the landscape. At least she confirmed that there was human life on this prairie.

Hours passed slowly. The heat must have reached one hundred degrees. Our water supply was about halfway gone. In the distance we could see a police cruiser approaching us from the west. We hoped he didn't see us, but he'd have to be blind to miss us. There were no trees or road signs to block his view. Sure enough, he had his sights focused on the two hippies standing in the breakdown lane on his highway.

He rolled up beside us and rolled down the window on our side. "What are you boys doing?"

Lewis must have been thinking the same thing I was. In my head was, "What does it look like, you dumbass?"

Without skipping a beat, Lewis applied his sarcastic charm and answered, "Oh, thank you for asking, officer.

We're just out for an afternoon stroll along this beautiful highway."

I couldn't hold back, and broke out laughing. Lucky for us, the officer had a sense of humor. He suppressed a smile and asked for identification. Lewis and I handed him our driver's licenses.

As he inspected our documents, he said, "You boys can't hitchhike here. You have to stay off the ole."

"What did you say?" I asked.

He repeated, "Stay off the ole."

I was about to ask, "What the hell is ole?" when Lewis intervened and said, "Yes sir, we'll stay off the oil." That's what they called the tar out here, or at least the breakdown lane.

"If I catch you on the ole again, I'll arrest you and bring you straight to jail."

Well OK! Maybe hitchhiking in Wyoming wasn't such a good idea, after all. Hitchhiking from twenty feet off the road, where the grass was high, would not help our cause—we'd be difficult to see. A half hour after the state trooper drove off, we were back on the *ole*, and keeping an eagle eye out for any approaching police cruisers.

NO SHIRT, NO SHOES, NO SERVICE

As the day wore on a few more pickup trucks with cowboys sped by, launching projectiles and some choice Wyoming vernacular at us. Lewis and I were tired of being abused. If we had the chance, we would have gladly punched one of those jerks in the nose.

At last, a station wagon slowed down and pulled even with us. We were both off the *ole* at that point, about twenty feet from the station wagon. Both Lewis and I weren't going to take any more abuse and were ready for a confrontation. The odds were in our favor—there was just one occupant in the vehicle. He beckoned us over. I could feel my anger swelling and adrenaline fueling fear in me as we approached the car.

In the driver's seat was an old man under a cowboy hat. With his tanned, leathery face with deep wrinkles, he didn't appear very threatening. This guy had had a life of hard work, and it showed on his face.

As he reached down beside himself to the passenger seat I readied myself to spring away from the car. Instead of a weapon, he lifted up a bag from McDonalds and offered it to Lewis. He explained that he had passed by us a couple of times and thought we might be down on our luck. So he decided to buy us lunch. He even offered to bring us to his ranch so we could get cleaned up. He'd bring us back to the highway afterward.

We thanked him profusely for the food. He wouldn't accept any money. We politely turned down his offer for the trip to his ranch, explaining that we needed to stay on the move as we had a very long way to go. As he drove off we just looked at each other. This gentle old man had restored our faith in humanity. After all the abuse we had endured that day, a saint had appeared.

To this day, that old man's benevolence still puts a lump in my throat. The lesson I learned from that one selfless act has been with me ever since.

We waited there for more long hot hours and then another vehicle stopped, but it wasn't a nice guy. It was the same Wyoming state trooper.

This time he ordered us into the patrol car and informed us he was taking us to jail back in Cheyenne. We pleaded with him and asked what we were supposed to do.

We needed to get back to Boston, and Boston was still two thousand miles away. He said he didn't care, but he did give us the opportunity to walk out of the state. We asked how far that was, and he said fifty miles. We accepted his offer. Any plan would be better than going to jail.

The trooper said he would come back and check on us. "If I catch you two on the highway one more time I promise I'll take you straight to jail."

This time we believed him. He let us out of the car and watched as we trudged back up the embankment, and started walking toward the Nebraska border. We should have asked how far to the next exit, but didn't.

We walked several miles this way. Sometimes the embankment came down level with the road, and we could stay at least twenty feet away from the highway. Awhile later we did see a state police car go by, but we couldn't tell if it was the same trooper.

Dusk arrived. We had been baking on the hot prairie all day and had advanced eastward only a few miles. Dispirited, we walked away from the highway into a field, jumped over a split rail fence and unrolled our bags to go to sleep. We didn't want to be in sight of traffic just in case some locals decided they might want to kill some sleeping hippies that night. The movie *Easy Rider* was only two years old, and we both remembered the brutal scene when locals beat the three rogue travelers with baseball bats.

CHAPTER 9

Morning came. When I first opened my eyes I was lying on my back and staring upward to find a horse staring down at me with her nostrils a few inches above mine. I felt an instant of panic, but managed to stay still. The fence we had climbed over the night before was evidently there to corral the herd. Another horse was about two feet from my face, grazing. A few others were scattered around, all ignoring us.

Lewis was already awake and sitting up. We quietly rolled up our sleeping bags and lifted our gear back over the fence. We sat midway between the highway and the fence and discussed our situation. We had no idea how far the next exit was, and there was no way we could walk another forty-five miles to the state border. Even if we did, we might get the same reception from a police officer in Nebraska.

We decided we had no choice but to risk being caught, so went down to the edge of the highway. It couldn't have been much later than 7 a.m. There weren't many travelers on the road. Cars would pass us at five to ten minute intervals. Rather than stand on the side of the road with our thumbs pointing east, we took turns standing in the center of the east bound lane screaming "Help!" at the passing traffic, hoping someone would take pity on us before the cops hauled us away. Lewis had a red windbreaker that he would wave around hoping to get people's attention. He got their attention all right, and was almost run over for his efforts by more than one driver. People just weren't going to stop and help us out.

Until, finally, one did.

It was an older model maroon four-door Oldsmobile 88 with a crack in the windshield. It came to a screeching stop beside us. We looked in the window and the driver motioned us to get in. Lewis swung open the passenger side door and froze. The driver was pointing a revolver right at Lewis' face. We both stood motionless for a moment until the driver said, "You boys look all right. Get in." And he tossed the gun in the glove compartment and slammed is shut. At this point we were willing to take a chance to put some miles behind us, so we threw our gear in the back seat and climbed in the front. There were two of us and one of him and the gun was closer to us than it was to him. It was worth the risk.

The driver looked to be in his sixties, medium build, with short-cropped thinning hair that was more salt than pepper. He had several days' worth of stubble, and his face was blotchy. He looked like he'd led a rough life. But to Lewis and me, a ride was a ride.

It didn't take us long to suspect that our host may not be sober. There was an empty bottle of Muscatel on the passenger side floor. He hadn't said a word to us. After a few minutes I asked him how far he was going. He only responded by pointing to the dashboard. After a few more minutes of awkward silence Lewis asked him the same question, and the guy just pointed to the dashboard again.

After a few more *very* awkward minutes, the old guy realized we hadn't understood his gestures and said, "I'll take you as far as you give me money for gas and wine." I replied that we didn't have much but we'd be happy to help pitch in a little and asked him again where he was headed. He replied he was going to Florida to "carve out a new life," so we said okay, and settled into an uneasy silence.

The car swayed as if it needed new shock absorbers. Or maybe our driver was that drunk. He looked at me and said, "Lets see how fast we can get this car going."

In front of us was a long, straight stretch of highway with meadowland on both sides. Nothing to crash into if the car went off the road. The Oldsmobile began to accelerate. I watched the speedometer needle climb and the road signs blur as we approached 110 miles per hour. The car seemed to top out at that speed and the driver took his foot off the gas—much to my relief.

About a half hour later, the old guy pulled over to the side of the highway and stopped the car. He got out, walked behind the car, then unzipped his pants and began to urinate. Lewis and I looked at each other as if to say, "Should we run away?" but we decided to stay and see how far we'd get.

The old guy got back in, thanked us for not stealing his car (he had left the keys in the ignition) and figured maybe we were okay after all. He asked us where we were going and we told him Boston. He said fine, and that he would take us there and then head south. I didn't try to convince him that it wasn't exactly the shortest path to Florida.

By this time we had covered the forty-five miles to the state line and crossed back into Nebraska. That Wyoming state trooper couldn't bother us here.

A few miles after we crossed state borders we came across two more hitchhikers. The old guy stopped to pick them up. Before they got in we told them, through an open window, that we needed gas and they'd have to agree to buy some if they wanted a ride. They readily accepted.

One of our new travel companions was a guy about forty. He had dark, neatly trimmed hair, and from a guy's perspective, was good looking. The other passenger was a skinny young guy with acne who looked about twenty or so. Neither one of them had any gear—no backpacks or suitcases. Lewis and I stuffed our backpacks into the trunk and the new guys got into the back seat. The older of the two asked the driver how far was he going and got the same answer—Florida.

Once we all settled, the old guy drove a few miles before he pulled off the highway to gas up. We stopped at a gas station and convenience store, and the *nouveau*

Floridian sat in the car as the new passengers gassed up his car and went into the store. They came out with a couple bags and got back in the car. They had purchased some potato chips and other snacks, some beer, and a bottle of Muscatel for the old guy. Muscatel is a sweet, fortified wine that is about forty proof. It's almost the same strength as a cocktail that is half whiskey half something else. We headed back onto the highway and the old guy opened his wine, took a pull, put the cap back on and set it between his legs. The dark haired guy in the backseat gave everyone else a beer and passed around the chips. It was only about ten in the morning, but what the heck. When in Rome, right?

We asked the two in the back where they were going and how did they wind up on the side of I-80 on a Friday morning? The older one, whom we later dubbed the Flim Flam man, and his protégé looked at us as if trying to figure out whether they could trust us or not. Realizing we were probably as destitute as they were, he told us that they had been in Cheyenne the night before. He had met a guy at a bar, got him drunk, beat him up, robbed him, and stole his car. They'd left the car up on the exit just before the state line and walked into Nebraska. He said that to take the car across state lines would be a federal offense. We didn't know if that was true, but it sounded believable. And we sure weren't about to call him a liar.

We kept driving. The old guy kept nipping on his bottle and the four of us were having a good time telling stories. Then the old guy asked us if we have any "of that there marijuana." We told him we did, and he said he sure wanted to try it.

Lewis rolled one up. I lit it, took a long drag on it, and then handed it to him. He passed it around some but kept most of it for himself, which, at 10 a.m., was fine with us.

A couple minutes later he declared, "This here marijuana sure makes me alert!"

A few minutes after that, the car began to swerve and he said, "Somebody's gotta drive!"

He pulled over and asked the Flim Flam man to drive, cautioning him that it was an old car that should not exceed 70 miles per hour. The two exchanged seats and off we went. The old guy fell asleep and the rest of us passed the time with small talk. We told the guys more about our adventure. The young one was impressed and wanted to hear all about it and where we were headed. After a few hours we stopped for gas again and the old guy woke up. We fueled up and had to look for a liquor store so we could buy him another bottle of Muscatel. At least the guy was a cheap drunk. We tossed the bottle of wine to him in the back seat and the rest of us got something to eat before getting back on the road.

Our two friends' destination was a small farming town not far off the highway. As the old guy slept in a drunken stupor in the backseat, we exited and followed a dusty dirt road toward an oasis of trees, farmhouses, and grain silos on the horizon. We had been swapping the driving responsibilities between the four of us and Lewis was the one behind the steering wheel.

Once we reached the trees and houses, Lewis stopped the car and a cloud of dust encircled us. It was steaming hot outside. We were on a tree-lined dirt road near a farmhouse. We said our goodbyes and good-lucks to our fellow travelers. They climbed out opposite back seat doors. Before we had a chance to drive away, the younger man knelt down next to my open window and asked, "What's it like back East?" As we drove away, it dawned on me that he'd probably never been much farther east than this town right here.

Lewis and I drove for a few more hours. We had left Wyoming, crossed most of Nebraska and were now approaching Iowa. By now it was close to dinnertime and both Lewis and I noted that the old guy hadn't eaten anything all day. He just drank his wine. When he did wake up and speak, he was getting a little weird. He spoke as if he thought we were going with him to Florida to help him carve out a new life down there.

We drove on for another two hours and saw signs for a rest area. Our host wanted us to pull in and park at the rest area for the night. He said he didn't want to overheat the old car and thought it was time to give it a rest. It was fine with us, so we pulled in and parked. Lewis and I took turns going into the restrooms, and then told him we were going to walk over to a grassy area, unroll our bags, get some sleep, and we'd see him in the morning. He curled up in the backseat and we walked away and sat down maybe fifty feet from the car.

We waited about thirty minutes, then walked down the rest area's ramp to the highway. The old guy was starting to freak us out and we wanted to get away from him.

Standing at the point where the ramp joined the highway, we were in view of both streams of traffic, and sure enough, a guy pulling out of the rest area picked us up and took us a few exits down the road. We got off at the top of the ramp, which was out in the country somewhere west of Des Moines, and found a spot to bed down for the night.

We had made good progress today compared to the disastrous day we'd had Thursday. We figured we'd gone about six hundred miles and had less than four hundred left to get to Chicago. We hoped we'd be there tomorrow night.

Saturday, September 4 was our first rainy day. Fortunately, we both had lightweight ponchos to keep us dry at the bottom of the ramp. The going was slow. It took till late morning just to get to the other side of Des Moines. We wondered if people were less inclined to pick up hitchhikers in the rain. After a bit, though, we got a good ride that took us to just outside of Davenport. Then things took a turn for the worse.

NO SHIRT, NO SHOES, NO SERVICE

We were standing at the bottom of the ramp when the wind really started to blow. It was raining sideways. We walked back under the bridge to get out of the driving rain, but the wind was blowing the rain almost horizontally. Then Lewis noticed a really odd thing on the prairie up past the ramp: It was a string of clouds that had come down from above, touched the ground, and started turning.

The wind had really picked up. About fifty feet away, there was a culvert that ran under the road. With the rain pelting us and the wind buffeting our backpacks, we ran there and crawled into the pipe for protection. It was kind of scary being *under* the highway and hearing the wind howling overhead. After ten minutes or so, the wind lessened and we crawled out of the culvert and went back under the bridge. We were soaked.

A short while later, an Iowa state trooper pulled up behind us, turned on his flashers, and got out of the patrol car and walked our way. Sure enough, we were under arrest again for hitchhiking on a controlled-access highway.

He drove us to a highway patrol station a few miles away. In the station they frisked us and went through our gear but didn't bother to strip-search us. That was a good thing, because we still had a little stash left. They didn't make us pay a fine, but did make us sit and wait awhile, just to punish us. After giving us a lecture, the trooper took us to the highway, dropped us off at the top of the ramp and said next time we wouldn't be so lucky.

At least it had stopped raining. By now it was dinnertime and there was a little restaurant, some kind of chicken place but not a Kentucky Fried, about two hundred feet away. We walked over and ate a hot meal, then walked back to the top of the ramp. By now it was getting close to dusk and we wondered if we should just bed down. Instead, we decided we might as well see if we could get a ride.

Before long, a stake truck went by with a bunch of kids in the back hooting and hollering at us. Maybe fifteen minutes later they came back and slowed down to take a look at us. They drove by, then turned around, came back and stopped. Not forgetting the people in Wyoming that threw beer bottles and firecrackers at us, we wondered if they were going to beat us up, or worse. The driver, who apparently was the leader of this little group, stepped out onto the road. With his friends, who by now had climbed down from the back, asked us what we were doing. He didn't seem belligerent, so we told him where we were from, where we'd gone, and that we were on our way to Chicago.

They appeared to be genuinely interested, so the apparent leader introduced himself as John, asked our names, then asked where we were going to sleep tonight. We pointed to a grassy spot maybe a hundred feet away and said we'd probably camp there. He asked if we wanted to go to a party, and told us that he and his friends were going to meet at a nearby field, camp out, make a big bonfire and drink homemade apple wine. This sounded more interesting than sleeping on the side of the road, and if they were going to kill us, we figured they'd have done it already. We piled into the back of the truck with the rest of the guys and drove off.

About fifteen minutes later we pulled off onto a dirt road, drove for a little bit, and then pulled into an open area where a number of pickup trucks and cars were parked. We got out with the rest of the guys, and John introduced us to the other twenty or so people there. The partiers were mostly guys, but a few girls were present. The group had already built a fire and was passing around pop bottles full of homemade apple wine. John called it apple jack. He warned us that the stuff was very potent and to take it easy. It didn't taste great, but was palatable.

Someone had brought a boom box to supply the music, and everyone started having a good time. Lewis and I regaled them with the exploits of our trip, and we definitely embellished some of the stuff. Especially the part about the bears and all the times we were arrested. When we got to the part about the tornado starting right next to us, one of the guys said, "Yeah, I heard something about that on TV at dinner," and Lewis somberly said, "Yep, we were very lucky to have lived through that," and we showed them the mud on our jeans that had come from hiding under the culvert. We felt like traveling stage troupe.

After a couple of hours people started wandering back to their vehicles and falling asleep or passing out. We unrolled our bags at the edge of the field, took care of business, and went to sleep.

CHAPTER 10

The next thing I knew, John was bending over me and hooting at the top of his voice in my ear. Startled, it took me a few seconds to remember where I was—but just who the heck was this guy screaming at me?

My head was pounding. I couldn't focus my eyes at first because the morning sun, still low on the horizon, was blinding me. In a moment it dawned on me that I wasn't dreaming. The memories of the previous evening explained why I was so hung over. This was not a good way to start the day. In fact, we were both hurting. Lewis and I got up, packed our stuff, and unsteadily climbed back into the truck. A lot of the vehicles had already left. Whether they left last night or this morning, we didn't know. And given our hangovers, we didn't care. We declined John's offer to stop to get something to eat; truth is, neither Lewis nor I felt much like looking at food. We said our goodbyes, and began a new day of hitchhiking.

We stayed at the top of the ramp for maybe an hour, and then a middle-aged man stopped and asked where we were going. We told him Chicago and he said that he couldn't take us that far but he would at least get us partway into Illinois. That was fine with us. We put our stuff in the backseat, and I got in front.

Along the way, my perception of everyday people had been evolving. That evolution may have started the first day of the adventure. From the police officers at the Massachusetts State Barracks who were keenly interested in our quest to climb mountains in the Rockies, to the jailor, who had probably witnessed some of humanity's worst delinquents, but could see that we weren't among them. The kids our age whom we camped with, like us, just wanted to have fun. The cop in Wyoming who gave us a second chance. We had met some good people—and most of all, the old cowboy who went out of his way to buy us some McDonald's hamburgers.

On the flip side, we had managed, by luck or instinct, to avoid getting hurt. The drug dealers in Chicago, the old man with the gun, the Flim Flam man. We could have been mugged, shot, and never heard from again. A fall at 14,000 feet, no drainpipe to crawl into during a tornado, getting hit by a car or a flying beer bottle—any of these mishaps could have changed the rest of our lives. Lady Luck was with us.

At the time, neither Lewis nor I knew it, but this summer had changed the rest of our lives. We shared experiences that few people would ever encounter. We had built up self-confidence and mental stamina. At eighteen, none of this had yet come to mind. But later in life, in dealing with the good and the bad, my experience on the road had a subliminal influence on how I approached adversity and other people.

Less than half an hour later we were in Illinois, and glad to leave Iowa behind. In Illinois we hitched from the bottom of the ramp, hoping that either there weren't as many police patrolling on a Sunday morning, or that they would at least give us a warning before taking us to jail.

We made good time that day, and our last ride brought us into the city of Chicago by early afternoon. We weren't as lucky as the last time we entered Chicago, when the parole officer brought us right to the entrance of Lake Point Tower. But we were only a few miles away. Rather than try to hitchhike in the city, we hailed a cab and were happy to finish this leg of the journey in comfort for only a couple dollars each. We were still mindful of the parole officer's stories of Cook County Jail, and we didn't think it would be wise to walk the city streets with our packs. And who knew what Chicago's finest would do to longhaired, dirty hitchhikers?

The cabbie dropped us off at the entrance to Lake Point Tower and we were happy to see the same doorman we had met several days before. The doorman didn't have a key for us and it was right then that we realized Lewis had not told his mother that we were on our way. In fact, it was amazing how little contact we'd had with our families for the last two weeks. I hadn't contacted mine since we'd last been in Chicago. Likewise, Lewis had not contacted anyone since Bob dropped us off on Interstate 80.

Lewis pleaded with the doorman, who told us to try the leasing office. "Even though it is Sunday," he said, "there is always someone in the office."

Lewis and I took his advice and walked into the building lobby. This time people *really* stared at us. We were filthy. Lewis's jeans looked like he'd gone through a war, and I'm sure we smelled just as bad. Nevertheless, Lewis approached an impeccably dressed young man and asked where the leasing office was. With a horrified look on his face the man blurted out, "The *leasing* office?" and backed up a step so as not to touch us. He pointed the way and abruptly left.

We found the office, and behind a desk was a pleasant woman in her fifties. Lewis introduced himself and explained our situation. Fortunately, the woman knew his mother and asks him some questions to verify his identity.

Then she said, "Under all that dirt I guess you look like your mother," and gave Lewis a spare key. We thanked her and headed for the elevators that serviced Sixty-Oh-One. The key worked and we were inside. This part of the trip was finally over.

Hunger was the driving force behind our first moments in civilization. In the refrigerator we found assorted cold cuts and cheese—enough to make some enormous sandwiches. Ignoring the dirt and grime we were probably painting all over the furniture, we sat down by the big windows and ate our fill.

While reminiscing, we recalled how difficult a time we had hitchhiking from Topsfield to Chicago. We both admitted that we were pretty sick of hitchhiking.

It's one thing to be heading out for a Great Adventure, quite another to face a thousand-mile trip to someplace as ordinary as home. We decided to find an alternative mode of transportation—some means that didn't involve standing on the side of the road, at the complete mercy of strangers.

We made several phone calls to bus companies and airlines. To our great surprise and pleasure we discovered that it only cost a dollar more to fly to Boston than to take a bus: forty-five dollars for a one-way flight from Chicago's O'Hare to Boston's Logan Airport seemed like a bargain. It was just a bit more than being thrown in jail. We decided to wait for Lewis's mother to return to make sure someone could take us to the airport, and then we'd book our flight.

I finally called home and told my mother that we were fine, that we'd had a great trip and were in Chicago. I explained that we were tired of hitchhiking and that we would be flying home tomorrow and asked if someone could pick us up at the airport—but if we had to hitchhike home from Logan Airport, we'd be okay with that, also. It wouldn't change our plans.

We hadn't considered the fact that tomorrow was Labor Day and that maybe everyone would be gone for the three-day weekend. Fortunately, that was not the case. Even though she was somewhat upset at not having heard from me for almost two weeks, she said that someone would meet us at the airport. She just needed the flight number and arrival time.

Lewis and I were eager to fly the rest of the way home, albeit the fact that it was sort of cheating. We'd done almost the whole trip with just our thumbs and wits. There were only eight hundred miles remaining to make it a complete loop. But both of us agreed: It was time to get cleaned up, and put hitchhiking behind us.

Lewis showered first, then me. While I was enjoying the warm water rinsing away the road dirt, Lewis started a load of laundry. As I emerged from the bathroom I was astonished to find him wearing a pair of blue bell-bottom pants with white buttons up the front and *no holes in the cloth.*

He said, "They might not let me on the plane with those jeans and I have been saving these for a special occasion." Once again, I playfully berated him about the fact that that we might have gotten here a lot faster if he'd worn his nice pants.

While gazing through the sixtieth-story windows, we had each melted into separate pieces of living room furniture and fallen asleep. The sound of an opening door awoke us. It was Lewis's mom and Bob.

They weren't surprised to see us. The doorman had told them that the two vagabonds had reappeared. They were glad to see us safely back in the civilized world. It really never occurred to us how worried our families might be by our traveling two-thirds the way across the country with nothing but the packs on our backs.

Bob said he'd be happy to drive us to O'Hare, so we booked our flight and finished up the laundry. I called my mother and let her know the details, and she said Dad would pick us up at Logan. Lewis called his dad and told him the same thing, and that he would be at Grandma's house tomorrow before dinner. Then, we ate a meal with Bob and Lewis's mom, happy to just stay at the apartment and not go anywhere.

NO SHIRT, NO SHOES, NO SERVICE

We told them most of the things that had happened. We left out the parts concerning police and apple jack. Lewis's mother kept saying over and over how glad she was that we were safe.

After Bob left, we spent some more time looking out over the city before we all turned in for the last night of our journey. The Chicago skyline reminded me of the Needle Mountain peaks in the San Juan Mountains. Chicago was a man-made canyon of concrete and steel, but it, too, reached toward the stars. My thoughts turned to a time that now seemed so distant; the nights we had spent camping under the stars above tree line between Twin Lakes were seared in my memory. So were the towering rock spires shielding the green and turquoise alpine lakes. Compared to the stars above Chicago Basin in the San Juan Mountain Range, the city lights had nothing on Mother Nature.

CHAPTER 11

We woke up early and got our gear together. Bob showed up, and after a light breakfast we headed for O'Hare in his 1969 Thunderbird.

When we arrived at the airport, we picked up our boarding passes and checked our packs. The attendant had to put them in cardboard boxes so our stuff wouldn't fall out on their way down the conveyor belt. After Bob was certain that we were all set, he shook our hands and took off for his office.

Soon, it was time to board. The plane was almost full and we had a window and a center seat. It's a fairly short flight, so I didn't mind sitting in the middle while Lewis got the window seat. In less than two hours, we were covering the distance it took us two and half *days* to traverse. As we flew out at thirty thousand feet we reminisced about what it was like to hitchhike from home to the top of a mountain. That feeling of sitting on top of the world gave me goose bumps once again. As it turned out, the mental picture I had of the jagged peaks, the alpine lakes, and the scattered patches of snow would have to sustain me. Unfortunately, the film in Lewis's 35 mm camera had not been loaded correctly, and by the time we discovered it the best of the trip was behind us.

Before we knew it, the no smoking and fasten seat belt lights came on and the flight attendants walked the length of the aisle, checking our trays and seat belts. We started the descent into Boston.

Our way out of the plane, we walked through the tunnel and saw my dad at the gate. He shook our hands, said how glad he is that we were back, and then reminded me how worried my mother had been.

"Next time, be sure you call more often."

I doubted that there would ever be a next time.

We descended the escalator to baggage claim, got our gear, then walked out to the parking lot and located my dad's car, a 1968 Camaro. I recognized it right away—it was Sea Breeze Green, according to General Motors, but when Dad brought it home for the first time, my brother and I agreed that it looked more like Trash Can Gray. Lewis jumped in the backseat with the packs, and I sat in front. The whole trip north, we were telling him all the stuff we went through, the good and the bad, how spectacular the mountains were and how good it felt to be back.

We got to Hamilton and dropped Lewis off. I got out of the car while he was getting his pack and we shook hands, and then pulled each other closer and slapped each other's back. We stood apart, still gripping each other's hand, just holding eye contact, speechless. I knew what he was thinking, and he knew what I was thinking. The journey of a lifetime was over.

When I arrived home, the whole family was excited to see me and hear about the trip. I tried to remember as much as I could, but already some of the details had started to slip away. It already was starting to feel like a dream. By now the realization was sinking in: It's over. My next mission in life was to begin college as a freshman in a few days.

I saw Lewis a couple more times before he headed off to East Lansing and Michigan State University. His Uncle Richard arranged for the Bumblebee to be towed to a garage and had the rear end fixed, so Lewis was able to load all his stuff and drive back out west. We hoped it wouldn't break down again.

Our adventure had ended.

Neither of us realized at that point what we had done. To us, it was simply an extended camping trip. As time passed and as times changed, however, I realized how special a time it was in my life. Today, it would be nearly impossible for two teenagers to do what we did.

I entered the University of New Hampshire that fall. Lewis went back to the Michigan State University. Our lives, separate now, took on the social and academic complexities of college life. Lewis's mom married Bob and moved to Nantucket Island where they opened up a high-end antique shop for the island elite, and a trinket store for the tourist trade.

I have seen Lewis only twice since that summer. He invited me to Nantucket when we were both college students. He was spending a summer between semesters on the island with Bob and his mom. Another time, several years later, he was traveling through the area after college with his new wife. After that, I only talked to him on the phone a couple of times over the next two years. Once was to tell him that our very good friend, Ricky

Evans, had died in a car crash. He wasn't very good at correspondence, and I eventually gave up trying. After that, we lost touch with each other.

But across the miles and the decades, we will always share the memories of that incredible journey in the summer of 1971.

STEVE COX ALSO WROTE

If You Love Me, Take Me Now

ONLINE IMAGES AND RESOURCES

all photos and materials © their respective owners

OLD NEEDLETON WATER TANK:
http://goo.gl/n8aITL

DURANGO-SILVERTON RAIL ROAD:
http://goo.gl/uKhgVy
http://goo.gl/88HFh7

TRAIL TO CHICAGO BASIN:
http://goo.gl/YQLUSG

TWIN LAKES:
http://goo.gl/K6ZLrU

NORTH VIEW FROM SUNLIGHT PEAK:
http://goo.gl/JIILJC

VIEWS FROM WINDOM PEAK:
http://goo.gl/yxhzHp
http://goo.gl/yzIVJV
http://goo.gl/1aWWy8

DANVERS STATE INSANE ASYLUM:
http://goo.gl/TgTJIS

www.ingramcontent.com/pod-product-compliance
Lightning Source LLC
Chambersburg PA
CBHW050537300426
44113CB00012B/2154